Collins

KEY STAGE 3

HISTORY

T0312374

BOOK 1: 1066-1750

ELIZABETH SPAREY, GRAHAM BERRY, PETER JACKSON, JO PEARSON

Published by Collins
An imprint of HarperCollins Publishers
The News Building
1 London Bridge Street
London
SE1 9GF

HarperCollins *Publishers*
1st Floor, Watermarque Building, Ringsend Road
Dublin 4, Ireland

Browse the complete Collins catalogue at
www.collins.co.uk

HarperCollins Publishers Limited 2010
15

ISBN 978 0 00 7345748

Commissioning Editors: Charlie Evans, Lucy McLoughlin
Project Editor: Tim Satterthwaite
Concept Design: EMC Design
Page Design: Ken Vail Graphic Design
Illustrations by David McAllister/NB Illustration, Ben Hasler/NB Illustration
Cover Design by Joerg Hartmannsgruber, White-Card
Production: Simon Moore
Printed and bound in the UK using 100% Renewable Electricity at CPI Group (UK) Ltd

With particular thanks to Natalie Andrews

MIX
Paper from
responsible sources
FSC C007454

Contents

Unit 5 Ordinary people in early modern England   184

1 What is history?

Questions

This photograph shows a family in Britain about 100 years ago.

1 What does it tell you about the family?
2 What does it not tell you about the family?
3 What questions could you ask about the people in the picture?

Key terms

Historian – someone who asks questions about the past and uses sources of evidence to answer them

Source of evidence – an object or piece of writing from the past that helps an historian answer his or her questions about the past

You have now begun to be an historian. Historians study the past. They ask questions about the past and they use sources of evidence, such as this photograph, to help them answer their questions. In the course of this book you will be asking more questions about the past, and learning how to answer them like an historian.

What is history?

This book is all about history. In this unit you will be finding out what historians mean by history!

Getting you thinking

Below is a picture of a famous individual in history. Do you recognise him? Write down five things that you know about him.

He is Henry VIII. He was a member of the Tudor family. As king of England he had six wives. He is so famous that rhymes have been written about him:

> Bluff King Hal was full of beans
> He married half a dozen queens
> For three called Kate they cried the *banns*
> And one called Jane, and a couple of Annes.

In Key Stage 2 you will have studied history. In this book you are going to find out even more about history.

- Discuss with your partner:

  How many famous historical people can you think of?

  How many famous historical events do you know about?

Banns: an announcement of marriage

As you study history at Key Stage 3 you will learn that history is about more than famous kings and queens. You will learn about the history of your local community, Britain, Europe and the rest of the world. You will learn how to place events into the correct order in which they happened. You are going to ask and answer questions about the past, study historical *sources* of evidence and learn about different opinions people have about history. By studying history you are going to understand the events and individuals that have made Britain the country that it is today and our world the way it is.

A good place to start off when you are finding out about history is with yourself. Everybody has their own history. This is a picture of Matthew Pinsent. He was a famous Olympic rower and won four gold medals at different Olympic games.

The BBC series 'Who do you think you are?' researched his family history in 2007. They discovered he was related to King Edward I of England who ruled England between 1272 and 1307. You never know who you might be related to until you find out about your family history. You could also find out about the history of your local area. A good place to start is the local museum.

Now it's your turn

1 Write a list of anything that you already know about history.
2 How do you think you could find out about your own family history?
3 Now find out something about your own family history or local area.

Check your progress

I can describe an event from history.
I can talk about some important people in history.
I can talk about what historians do, and about historical sources.

Source: an object or a piece of writing from the past that helps an historian to answer his or her questions about the past

What is chronological history?

History isn't all about dates, but an important part of understanding history is knowing the order in which events happened.

Getting you thinking

It is important for historians to know when events in history happened. Look at the photograph below of York Minster.

Discuss in groups:
- How long ago do you think this building was built?
- What can we learn about the beliefs of the people who built this? (Clues: think about the size of the building, the decoration, the skills needed to make it and the cost.)

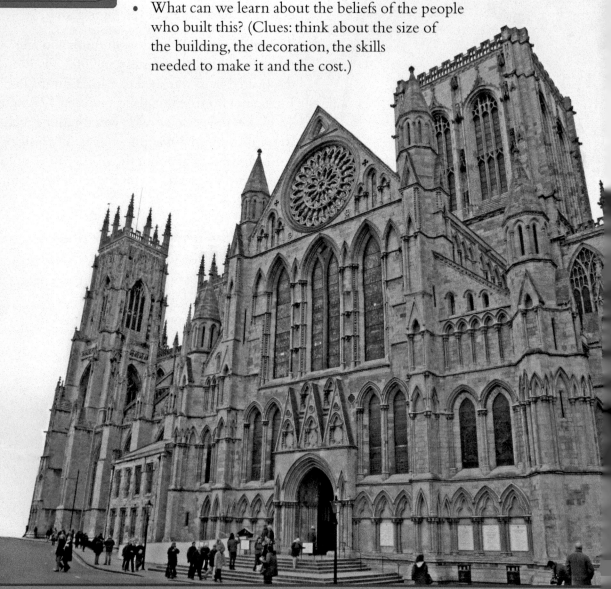

Anachronism: *an object which appears in the chrong time period*
BCE: *Before Common Era*

You need to be able to explain when events in the past took place. Historians use timelines to put events into the correct time order – their *chronological order*. If you study the timeline below you will see that 500 *BCE* happened before 200 *CE*. BCE means Before Common Era and refers to the years before Jesus was born. CE stands for Common Era and refers to the years since the time of Jesus.

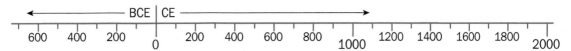

You will study many different periods of history at Key Stage 3. Below are six different time periods of history. See if you can sort the time periods into the correct chronological order.

- 20th century
- Medieval
- Anglo-Saxons
- Tudors and Stuarts
- Romans
- Industrial Revolution

As you find out more about history you will be able to recognise which objects come from which time period. During the Hollywood film *Ben Hur*, which is about Roman chariot racing, one of the actors can be seen wearing a wrist watch! An object which is described in a time it would not be found in is called an *anachronism*. For example, you would not find a mobile phone in Ancient Greece but you would find one today.

Now it's your turn

1 Draw your own timeline from 200 BCE to 200 CE. Write the following events on it:
   The death of Julius Caesar in 44 BCE
   The eruption of Mount Vesuvius in 79 CE
   Slave rebellion led by Spartacus in 73 BCE
   Death of Emperor Augustus in 14 CE
2 Sort the following into the correct time periods in history:
   - A World War One tank
   - King Alfred
   - Julius Caesar
   - Battle of Hastings
   - A Viking longship
   - The Black Death (Plague)
   - Queen Victoria
   - Henry VIII
   - A gladiator
   - A dishwasher
   - Gunpowder Plot
   - Invention of the steam train
3 Write a list of objects that exist today that would not have existed in 1945.

Check your progress

I can put some events into chronological order.
I can draw a timeline and put key events into their correct order.
I can show which events happen in different periods in history.

CE: Common Era
Chronological order: putting events into the order they happened

Which events happened during the lifetime of Harry Patch?

Objectives

By the end of this lesson you will be able to:

- put events into the correct chronological order

Now that you have begun to understand chronology, you are going to look at the lifetime of one man who died, aged 111, in 2009.

Getting you thinking

This is a photograph of World War One veteran Harry Patch. Harry was born on 17 June 1898 in Coombe Down, Somerset. He died on 25 July 2009. Harry was known as 'the Last *Tommy*', because when he died he was the last British person to have fought in World War One (1914–1918).

Tommy: a nickname given to British soldiers

Discuss with a partner: how many events can you think of which took place during Harry Patch's lifetime?

Harry joined the British Army in 1916 and began his training. He fought at the Battle of Passchendaele in 1917. He was injured on 22 September 1917 when a *shell* exploded near him. This explosion killed three of his friends. In 1918, World War One ended and Harry married his first wife, Ada. She died in 1976. After World War One, Harry worked as a plumber. He was too old to fight in World War Two (1939-1945), but he worked during this war as a part-time fireman in Bath. In 1980, Harry married his second wife who was called Jean. She died in 1984. In 2007, Harry wrote his autobiography with writer Richard van Emden. It was called *The Last Fighting Tommy*.

Just before Harry Patch died he was the oldest man in Europe. He outlived another World War One veteran, Henry Allingham, by just one week. Henry Allingham was 113 years old when he died, and had fought in World War One in the Royal Navy Air Service.

Harry Patch's funeral took place on Thursday 6 August 2009 in Wells Cathedral. It was broadcast live on TV and radio.

Now it's your turn

1 Draw a timeline from 1898 to 2009 and put on it as many events as you can from the life of Harry Patch.
2 Now put onto the timeline any other events you can think of that took place during Harry Patch's lifetime.
3 How much do you think life changed during Harry Patch's lifetime?

Putting events into the correct chronological order helps make sense of history. Find out how old Harry Patch was when the following events happened:
- Death of Queen Victoria (1901)
- Outbreak of World War Two (1939)
- Neil Armstrong walking on the Moon (1969)
- The September 11 terrorist attacks (2001)

Check your progress

I can put some events into chronological order.
I can draw a timeline of key events in the twentieth century.
I can show which events happen in different periods in history.

Shell: an explosive fired from an artillery gun

How different are people in the past and present?

Objectives

By the end of this lesson you will be able to:

- understand that people in the past and today are all different
- give reasons for why people have moved to Britain and other countries

History isn't just about chronology. It also helps you to understand about people with different lifestyles and beliefs. It helps you understand that people in the past were different from people now.

Getting you thinking

Think back to the people you have learnt about already in history. You might have learnt about Greeks, Romans or Tudors in Key Stage 2.

- How different do you think people were in the past from people today?

Diversity: when people are different

In fact, no two people are really the same. People have different hobbies, different places to live, different religions and different backgrounds. Read the source below from former Prime Minister Tony Blair:

We celebrate the *diversity* in our country, get strength from the cultures and the races that go to make up Britain today.

Source 1 *Former Prime Minister Tony Blair, 2 October 2001*

Tony Blair was saying that Britain is made up of many people of different races, religions and cultures. In fact Britain has always been a country made up of many different races and cultures. Early on in its history it was invaded by Romans, Anglo-Saxons, Vikings and Normans. Many people have come to Britain as *refugees* to escape wars and famines in their home countries. After World War Two people from countries like the West Indies, India and Pakistan were encouraged to come to Britain by the British government to work. Many people have also decided to leave Britain and start a new life in other countries such as the USA, Canada, Australia and Spain.

On the left is a photograph taken during the Notting Hill Carnival. The carnival has taken place every August since 1966. It began as a local festival organised by the West Indian community of London. Nowadays, it is one of the largest street festivals in Europe and people from different cultures and races enjoy the street party. It is a good example of what it means to live in a country made up of lots of different people.

Now it's your turn

1 Study the picture. What is the Notting Hill Carnival? Can you tell from the photo?
2 What message does the picture give about diversity in Britain?
3 Give some reasons why people decide to come to Britain.
4 Give some reasons why people would decide to leave Britain.
5 What impact do you think people moving into and leaving Britain have had throughout Britain's history?

Check your progress

I can describe some differences between people from different periods of history.

I can name some of the peoples who invaded Britain in its early history.

I can talk about some of the reasons why people came to live in Britain in the twentieth century.

Refugee: a person leaving their country to escape ill-treatment or famine

How much has Britain changed in the last 100 years?

Diversity is about differences between people, but history also helps you to understand about other differences. Change is about differences between different times in history. Historians also look for *continuity*, meaning things that have not changed and remain the same.

Getting you thinking

Thirsk is a market town in North Yorkshire. It is mentioned in the *Domesday Book* and has a weekly market that started in medieval times. Its name comes from a Viking word meaning marsh. Thomas Lord, who founded Lords cricket ground in London, was born in Thirsk.

The photograph above was taken around the year 1900. It shows market day in Thirsk and the time is midday (look at the clock). Monday has been market day in Thirsk as far back as records go and still is today.

Discuss: What can you learn from this photograph about life in Thirsk in 1900?

Continuity: when things stay the same

In 1900, the main form of transport was still the horse. Most pubs had stables for the horses. The railway had been invented and towns, including Thirsk, had train stations. Although the car had been invented, most people did not own one. Queen Victoria was still the Queen of England, having ruled since 1837. Britain was fighting a war in South Africa called the South African or Boer War. All children had to go to school from the age of 5 to around 12. Healthcare was slowly improving and children born in 1900 could expect to live well into their 50s. The population of Britain in 1900 was around 37 million.

Below is a photograph of Thirsk taken in 2009. Much of Thirsk has changed but you can still recognise the town. There is continuity, as well as change.

Now it's your turn

1 Study the two photographs.
  Write a list of what has stayed the same between 1900 and today.
  Write a list of changes that you can see between 1900 and today.
2 What do you think has changed the most between 1900 and today?
3 How much do you think life has changed between 1900 and today?

Check your progress

I can talk about some changes between 1900 and today.
I can use photographs as a source of historical evidence.
I can find examples of continuity and of change over the last hundred years.

How can sources help historians answer their questions?

Objectives

By the end of this unit you will be able to:

- give examples of the kind of questions historians ask
- explain what historians mean by the word 'source'
- explain how historians use sources

Historians ask questions about the past, but where do they find answers? Like detectives, they look for evidence. They find it in documents, objects and other kinds of sources.

Getting you thinking

Below is a photograph of the town of Pompeii in Italy. Pompeii is near the sea and near a volcano called Mount Vesuvius. Historians might ask: What happened to Pompeii on 24 August 79CE?

- Discuss with your partner: What questions do you need to ask to find out what happened to Pompeii?

You are going to look for evidence in sources to find out what happened in Pompeii.

The cloud was rising from a mountain – at such a distance we could not tell – but afterwards learned that it was Vesuvius. I can best describe its shape by comparing it to a pine tree. Broad sheets of flame were lighting up many parts of Vesuvius. The buildings were rocked by a series of strong tremors. Then came a smell of sulphur and flames.

Source 2 *Written in 79 CE by Pliny. He was a young Roman who was across the bay from Pompeii on the day the volcano erupted*

Source 1 *A photograph of Pompeii taken in the 21st century*

Source 3
Plaster casts made from the shapes of bodies, preserved in the volcanic ash, of people who died in Pompeii

On the morning of 24 August 79CE the pressure of the gases finally blew out the plug. Millions of tonnes of lava, pumice and ash were rocketed into the sky. They formed a great column 20 kilometres high, topped by a mushroom-shaped cloud. The cloud drifted south, right over Pompeii, where the fallout was worst.

Source 4 *From* Pompeii *by Peter Connolly (1990)*

Now it's your turn

1 What can you learn from each source about what happened at Pompeii on 24 August 79CE?
2 Look at Source 4. What can you learn from this source about what might have happened to the man in Source 3?
3 Which of the sources helps answer your enquiry the best?
4 Why do you think the town still remains for us to see today?
5 Imagine somebody in the future is writing your life story:
   • Write down a list of sources they could use to find out about you.
   • Which of the sources do you think they would find the most helpful for finding out about you?

Check your progress

I can use different sources to find out about history.
I can use sources to talk about the events in Pompeii.
I can talk about some of the different kinds of sources used by historians, and the ways they are used.

How do we know what is significant in history?

Getting you thinking

In 2002, the BBC ran a television programme called *Great Britons* to find out who has been the most important individual in British history. The winner was Winston Churchill for the part he played in helping Britain to win World War Two. Who would you choose?

History is a very big subject because it includes everything that has ever happened. Therefore, it is important for historians to be able to judge which events and individuals are *significant* and worth finding out about. A historian called Geoffrey Partington had several ideas about what significance means. Here are some of them:

- The people living at the time thought it was very important.
- It changed things very much for people living at the time and made their lives different.
- It affected a lot of people's lives.
- It affected people's lives for a long time.
- It affects our lives today.

Significant: important

Here are five individuals who were important in the 20th century.

Winston Churchill (1874–1965)

He was Prime Minister of Britain during World War Two. Many people think his famous speeches and strong leadership helped Britain win World War Two. He was Prime Minister again in the 1950s and when he died was given a state funeral.

Emily Davison (1872–1913)

She campaigned for women to get the vote. She threw herself in front of the king's horse at the 1913 Derby to highlight the unfairness of women not having the vote. Tragically, she died. Women eventually got the vote in 1918.

Alexander Fleming (1881–1915)

He was a Scottish scientist who discovered penicillin. Penicillin treats infections and became known as the wonder drug of the 20th century. The drug has saved millions of lives.

John Logie-Baird (1888–1946)

He was an inventor who created the world's first working television in 1926. Television now spans the globe and is the most popular form of entertainment in the world.

John Lennon (1940–1980)

He was a musician and member of The Beatles, who are widely regarded as one of the greatest bands there has ever been. He was also a peace activist campaigning against wars in the 1970s.

Now it's your turn

1. Study each individual and decide what makes them significant.
2. Hold a balloon debate. Imagine only one of the five key individuals can stay in the balloon. Decide which one of the five individuals is the most significant and why.
3. Who do you think is the least significant of the five individuals and why?

Check your progress

I can talk about some signficant people in British history.
I can decide which individuals were most significant, and give reasons.
I can talk about how historians judge whether a person or event is significant.

Causes and consequences of events in history

One of the skills you will develop when learning about history is to understand why events in the past have happened. Historians study the causes of events to explain why they happened. They also study what happened next. They call this the *consequences* of the event.

Getting you thinking

Can you think what kinds of events historians like to study?

This is a picture of the Gunpowder *Plotters*, including Guy Fawkes (named 'Guido Fawkes' in the picture). What do you already know about him?

Consequence: what happens after an event
Plotters: the men involved in organising the Gunpowder Plot

You probably know that Guy Fawkes was involved in the Gunpowder Plot. This was an attempt on 5 November 1605 to blow up the Houses of Parliament. The Gunpowder Plot was organised by a man called Robert Catesby. Guy Fawkes was just one of the plotters.

Historians are interested in finding out why the plotters wanted to blow up the Houses of Parliament.

Below are some clues.
- The plotters wanted to change the religion of England.
- 5 November 1605 was the opening of Parliament. Important Protestant people who ran the country would be there and Catholic Guy Fawkes wanted to kill them.
- King James I was going to be at the opening of Parliament and Guy Fawkes wanted to kill him.
- Guy Fawkes was asked to blow up the Houses of Parliament by Robert Catesby.
- Guy Fawkes was a successful soldier, experienced in dealing with explosives.

What were the consequences of the Gunpowder Plot? The plotters, including Guy Fawkes, were all executed. King James I wanted to make sure there were no more events like this. People were encouraged to light bonfires to celebrate the plotters being caught. By the 1700s it was popular to burn a 'guy' on top of a bonfire. Nowadays, people celebrate 'bonfire night' with bonfires and fireworks. This is all because of Guy Fawkes's actions on 5 November 1605.

Robert Catesby

Now it's your turn

1 Give some reasons why Guy Fawkes tried to blow up the Houses of Parliament.
2 Look at all the different reasons. Which do you think is the most important reason why Guy Fawkes tried to blow up the Houses of Parliament?
3 What do you think were the consequences of Guy Fawkes's actions?
4 There are many famous poems about Guy Fawkes. Write your own poem to remember what Guy Fawkes did on 5 November 1605.

Check your progress

I can describe some of the causes of the Gunpowder Plot.
I can describe some of the consequences of the Gunpowder Plot.
I can show how different causes linked together to make Guy Fawkes try to blow up the Houses of Parliament.

Houses of Parliament: the building where the important people who run the country meet to make decisions

Why do people have different opinions about the past?

Objectives

By the end of this lesson you will be able to:

- explain what is meant by an opinion
- give examples of why people have different opinions

Sometimes two historians ask the same question but come up with a different answer! history isn't just about facts. It is about opinions or *interpretations* of the past. You will need to understand why there are different opinions about the past.

Getting you thinking

Have you ever had a different opinion from somebody else? You might like a particular football team or type of fashion and somebody else might not. This is called having an opinion about something.

You are going to find out about the different opinions regarding Dr Alexander Fleming's part in producing the medicine penicillin.

First read these two interpretations about the discovery of penicillin.

Interpretation 1

"The man who made possible the discovery of penicillin is Dr Alexander Fleming. It will be hard to say who the great men of the twentieth century are, but Dr Alexander Fleming is certainly one of them."

Lord Beaverbrook, 1956

Interpretation 2

"Fleming told me often that he did not deserve the credit for penicillin, and I had to bite my teeth not to agree with him."

Dr W E van Heuningen, 1980

Interpretation: the meaning a person gives to an event

- Who does the first interpretation say did important work in developing penicillin?
- What does the second interpretation say about the discovery of penicillin?

As you read the following account, try to decide how the writer of each interpretation formed his opinion.

In 1928 Dr Alexander Fleming was studying a germ that caused spots. He grew the germ in dishes. Fleming was untidy and left the dishes in his laboratory before going on holiday. When he returned he noticed that a mould which had grown on the dishes had killed the germs. The mould was called *penicillium*. Fleming wrote a report on his discovery and then returned to his other work.

Later, two men called Howard Florey and Ernst Chain followed up Fleming's discovery. Florey had read Fleming's report. They worked out how to make enough penicillin to use as a medicine to treat people. They tried out the medicine on mice, then on a policeman. They discovered penicillin could cure many diseases. The US government thought their work so important that they paid for factories and equipment to make penicillin. The drug was developed quickly because it was needed to cure sick soldiers in World War Two.

A photograph of Dr Alexander Fleming

Now it's your turn

1 What evidence could be used to support interpretation 1?
2 What evidence could be used to support interpretation 2?
3 Which interpretation seems more convincing?

Check your progress

I can talk about how penicillin was discovered.
I can describe different opinions about who discovered penicillin.
I can use these different opinions to form my own opinion, and give reasons.

So, what is history?

You have now looked at a range of historical ideas and thought about how historians go about their work. Do you have you a clearer idea of what is meant by 'history'?

Getting you thinking

This is a photograph of Barack Obama.

In 2008, Obama was elected 44th President of the United States of America, the first African American ever to hold the post. People called his election historic. Historians in the future will study Barack Obama and what he achieves as President of the USA.

- What questions will historians ask about Barack Obama?

In the future, historians will ask questions about Obama using sources of evidence to study his achievements. They will study the reasons why he was elected and the consequences of his actions. Historians will form different interpretations about him and judge how significant he was. As the first African American President they will consider his impact on the cultural and ethnic diversity of the USA. As you see, history is not stuck in the past – it is happening all the time.

You have now found out about skills and ideas you need to be good at history. Throughout this book you are going to practise these skills in order to make progress.

Chronological understanding

You will be able to recognise the order in which events have happened and what it was like in different periods of history.

Cultural, ethnic and religious diversity

You will understand that people in the past and present are all different. The lives of medieval villagers and medieval townspeople were very different.

Cause and consequence

You will explain why events in the past took place and what the results were. For example, you are going to find out the reasons why Henry VIII divorced his first wife and the consequences of that divorce.

Significance

You will judge the significance of events. For example, was the English Civil War more important than Henry VIII in changing the English church?

Change and continuity

You will understand how much changed between 1066 and 1750 and how much stayed the same.

Interpretations

You will look at the different opinions historians have about history. For example, you are going to find out whether King Richard I really was a 'lionheart'.

Using sources of evidence

You are going to use sources of evidence to answer your own questions about the past. You will do some work where you set your own questions.

Now it's your turn

1 Look at the headlines in today's news.
2 Which events do you think historians in the future might study? Explain your choice.
3 What questions might historians in the future ask about today's events?

Check your level – have you?

I can describe some of the questions future historians might ask about Barack Obama.

Level 3

I can talk about what historians do, and why they sometimes have different opinions.

Level 4

I can suggest some events of our own time that will seem important to future historians.

Level 5

② Who had power in the Middle Ages?

Objectives

By the end of this unit you will be able to:

- describe the powers of the king and the church in the Middle Ages

- explain the reasons why the king and the church were powerful

- describe changes in power in the Middle Ages

- compare the power of rulers in England and in Muslim countries

This picture shows a very shocking event. Four knights are killing the most important churchman in England. He is the Archbishop of Canterbury. The knights are doing this because they think this is what the king wants them to do. What does it tell us about power in the Middle Ages? There are two powerful people involved: the king and the Archbishop of Canterbury. They represent the power of the monarchy and the power of the Roman Catholic Church. There had been a very serious quarrel between them. The quarrel was about power.

Key terms

Monarchy a way of ruling a country with a king or queen

Questions

1 Can you see the knights?
2 Can you see the Archbishop of Canterbury?
3 Who seems to have more power, the king's knights or the Archbishop of Canterbury?

What decided who held power in the Middle Ages?

The first part of this book is about the people who ruled England from 1066 until 1500. You will ask questions about who ruled, how they ruled, and how this changed during this long period of history.

Getting you thinking

The Middle Ages is the period from 1066 to around 1500 in English history.

In 1066 William, Duke of Normandy, invaded England to claim the throne that had been promised to him by King Edward the Confessor. He won it at the Battle of Hastings, defeating Harold Godwinson, the last Anglo-Saxon king. The period ended in 1485 when Henry Tudor defeated Richard III at the Battle of Bosworth. This ended the Wars of the Roses, a civil war between the Yorkists and Lancastrians.

- What does this tell you about what decided who became *monarch* in the Middle Ages?

Now it's your turn

Study the timeline on the opposite page and read the information about changes in who ruled.
- List different reasons that decided who became monarch in the Middle Ages. Give examples.
- Explain what was unusual about the reigns of Henry VI and Edward IV.

Check your progress

I can describe one way in which a monarch came to power in the Middle Ages.
I can describe several reasons why the ruling monarch changed.
I can give examples to explain how monarchs took the throne.

Monarch: a king or queen

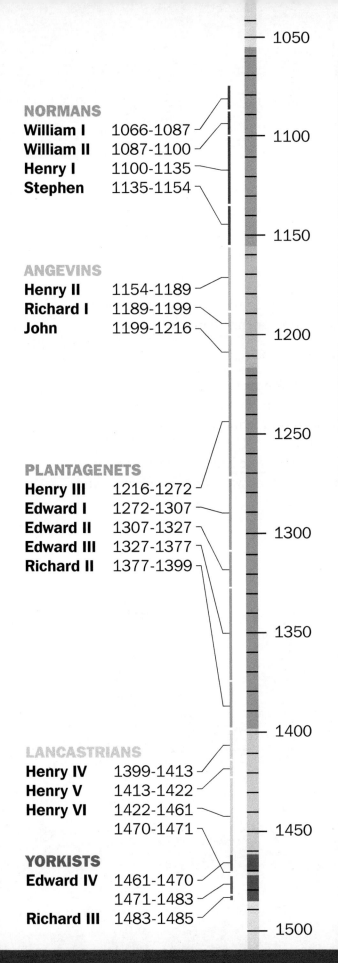

NORMANS
William I	1066-1087
William II	1087-1100
Henry I	1100-1135
Stephen	1135-1154

ANGEVINS
Henry II	1154-1189
Richard I	1189-1199
John	1199-1216

PLANTAGENETS
Henry III	1216-1272
Edward I	1272-1307
Edward II	1307-1327
Edward III	1327-1377
Richard II	1377-1399

LANCASTRIANS
Henry IV	1399-1413
Henry V	1413-1422
Henry VI	1422-1461
	1470-1471

YORKISTS
Edward IV	1461-1470
	1471-1483
Richard III	1483-1485

(Timeline: 1050, 1100, 1150, 1200, 1250, 1300, 1350, 1400, 1450, 1500)

Succession

Most kings were the eldest son of the previous king. There were exceptions! For example:

- William I left Normandy to his eldest son, Robert, and gave England to his middle son, William Rufus.
- Stephen was the nephew of King Henry I. Henry's sons drowned at sea. Henry left the throne to his daughter, Matilda. But the barons did not want a female ruler. She was never crowned queen.

Civil wars

These took place when there was disagreement about who had the best claim to the throne.

There were two major civil wars in the Middle Ages:

- Matilda v Stephen 1139–1148
- The Wars of the Roses 1455–1487

Coronation

It was important for a new monarch to be crowned by the Archbishop of Canterbury. This gave God's approval. Henry I was crowned just three days after his brother died. He wanted to make sure that his elder brother, Robert, did not claim the throne!

Murder

There were several possible murders. For example:

- William II was 'accidentally' shot by an arrow while hunting in the New Forest.
- Richard III may have murdered his nephews, the sons of Edward IV, known as 'the Princes in the Tower'.

What was power based on in the Middle Ages?

Objectives

By the end of this lesson you will be able to:

- describe ways of gaining power in the Middle Ages
- weigh up the evidence to reach a judgement about methods of gaining power

There was more to power than becoming king. A king also had to keep his throne. You are going to find out how kings did this in the Middle Ages.

Getting you thinking

If you want to make somebody do what you want, is it better to use force or get them to co-operate with you?

- Which way do you think is better?

The Norman cathedral at Durham was begun in 1093 to replace a Saxon church. William had promised the Pope he would make changes like this in return for his support. The cathedral stands next to the castle. The castle building was begun by William I in 1072 after he had crushed a rebellion in the north. The Bishop of Durham was a Prince Bishop, ruling the surrounding lands for the king.

Source 1 *Durham Cathedral*

Source 2 *Edward I's coronation 1272*

Edward I was crowned by the Archbishop of Canterbury. The coronation gave God's blessing to the reign. It was important, therefore, that Matilda was never crowned Queen of England. Can you remember why Henry I rushed his coronation? From the time of Henry I, monarchs swore a coronation oath in which they promised rights to their powerful subjects. Why do you think they did this?

Source 3 *The parliament of Edward I 1295*

Kings had always called a council of their powerful nobles and church leaders to help them rule. Parliament developed when rich merchants from towns and knights from the shires were added to the council. It became known as a parliament from the French word 'parler' (to talk). Parliament voted taxes and passed laws to help a monarch rule.

Source 4 *Battles*

Monarchs sometimes had to fight battles for their right to the throne. Can you remember who became king after Hastings in 1066 and Bosworth Field in 1485?

Some battles were fought between monarchs and barons! King John had to fight his barons. After defeating King Henry III, Baron Simon de Montfort even ran the country for a time.

Now it's your turn

In the MiddleAges a king's power was based on both force and cooperation.
1 Using the sources, make a list of all the ways that you can find force and cooperation being used by a monarch.
2 Where possible, add examples to explain how force and cooperation were used.
3 Which do you think was more important for a king to be strong – force or cooperation?

Check your progress

I can give an example of a king using force during the Middle Ages.

I can give examples of how kings used both force and co-operation to stay in power.

I can talk about why kings might have needed to use both force and co-operation.

1066 and the Norman Conquest: Who was to be the next king?

Objectives

By the end of this lesson you will be able to:

- give reasons why there was disagreement about who should be king in 1066

The Middle Ages, in England, started with a king winning his throne in battle. First you need to know why the other methods of deciding who had power were not used.

Getting you thinking

What rules do we have today about who should be the next king or queen?

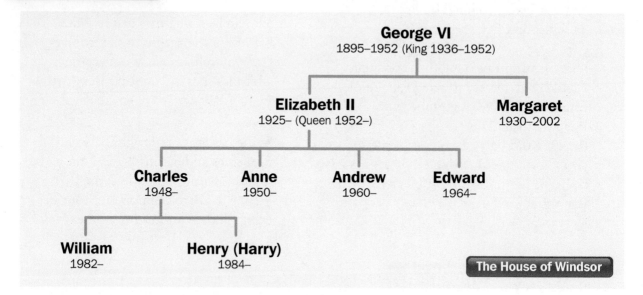

George VI
1895–1952 (King 1936–1952)

Elizabeth II
1925– (Queen 1952–)

Margaret
1930–2002

Charles
1948–

Anne
1950–

Andrew
1960–

Edward
1964–

William
1982–

Henry (Harry)
1984–

The House of Windsor

What was the problem in 1066?

In January, 1066, Edward the Confessor, King of England, died. But the rules were not the same as today.

The rules said that the new king should be a *blood relative* of the royal family.	**But**	… Edward the Confessor had no children and his nephew, Edgar was far too young.
The king had the right to choose his successor.	**But**	… Edward had promised the throne to two people.
The country needed a strong, experienced warrior king.	**But**	… in 1066 there were three men who were strong, experienced warriors who wanted to be king.

Blood relative: a relative of the royal family by birth

Harold Godwinson, Earl of Wessex

- The most powerful English noble
- Married to King Edward's sister
- Promised the English throne by Edward many times, including on his deathbed
- Had successfully governed England during Edward's reign

Harald Hardraada, the Viking king of Norway and Denmark

- Had the support of Tostig, Harold Godwinson's brother and an important English earl
- His ancestor King Canute ruled England from 1016 to 1035 so Hardraada believed he was heir to the English throne

William Duke of Normandy

- Was a distant relative of Edward the Confessor.
- Believed that he had been promised the English throne by Edward in 1051
- Edward had grown up in Normandy and loved William like a brother
- Said that Harold Godwinson promised to help him become king of England
- Had the support of the Pope, the head of the church

Now it's your turn

When Edward the Confessor died in 1066 the *Witan* met to agree on the next king. What would your opinion have been? Remember the rules!

1 Who is the best person to be the next king in 1066?
2 Why should the others not be the next king?

Check your progress

I can describe some of the problems facing England in 1066.

I can name the three men who wanted to be king in 1066.

I can describe some of the reasons why they each thought they should be king.

Witan: council of nobles and churchmen who advised the king

The events before the Battle of Hastings

Each of the three claimants to the throne was determined to be king. Now you are going to find out why it was William who became king.

Getting you thinking

Things can go well because you are lucky or because you make good decisions. Can you think of a time when you have been lucky or made a good decision?

Read about the events before the battle of Hastings and try to decide when luck helped William and when decisions helped him.

Events before the Battle of Hastings

1 In January Edward the Confessor died. The Witan chose Harold Godwinson as king. He was crowned on 6 January. On 24 April a *comet* was seen in the sky. Could this be a sign of bad luck for Godwinson?

2 Soon, William and Hardraada were planning to invade England. Who would arrive first? Godwinson split his army. Some waited in the south for William. Some waited in the north for Hardraada.

William was delayed by winds blowing the wrong way. On 8 September Godwinson sent the peasants in his southern army home to gather in the harvest. His fleet returned to the Thames.

Now it's your turn

Harold was about to go into battle with William, a battle he would lose. Look at what had happened so far to decide if William was luckier than Harold or made better decisions.

1 Draw and complete a grid like the following:

Godwinson's bad luck	William's good luck	Godwinson's bad decisions	William's good decisions

2 Which do you think has been more important so far, luck or decisions?

Comet: an object in the night sky, like a star with a long tail of light

3 On 18 September Hardraada landed in Yorkshire with 300 ships full of soldiers. He was joined by Godwinson's brother, Tostig. Hardraada defeated the northern English army at Fulford, near York, on 20 September.

On 21 September Godwinson marched north to face Hardraada, gathering troops on the way. On 25 September he surprised Hardraada at Stamford Bridge. Hardraada and Tostig were defeated. One rival to William had been removed with consequences – defeated. One rival to William had been removed and the English army had suffered heavy losses.

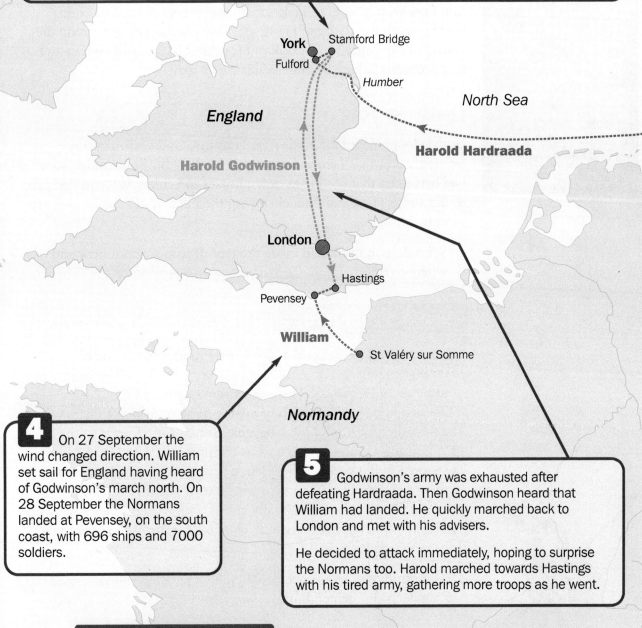

York

Stamford Bridge

Fulford

Humber

North Sea

England

Harold Hardraada

Harold Godwinson

London

Hastings

Pevensey

William

St Valéry sur Somme

Normandy

4 On 27 September the wind changed direction. William set sail for England having heard of Godwinson's march north. On 28 September the Normans landed at Pevensey, on the south coast, with 696 ships and 7000 soldiers.

5 Godwinson's army was exhausted after defeating Hardraada. Then Godwinson heard that William had landed. He quickly marched back to London and met with his advisers.

He decided to attack immediately, hoping to surprise the Normans too. Harold marched towards Hastings with his tired army, gathering more troops as he went.

Check your progress

I can give an example of how luck helped William.

I can give examples of how luck and good decisions helped William.

I can weigh up which was more important in helping William, and give reasons.

Why did William win the Battle of Hastings?
Part 1

You have seen how both luck and decisions contributed to events leading up to the Battle of Hastings. Now you are going to study the course of the battle itself. Look out for times in the battle when luck and decisions helped to cause William's victory.

Getting you thinking

Both sides prepared for battle near Hastings. Godwinson's army formed a *shield wall* around the top of Senlac Hill. Some of his men had battleaxes that could cut down horses and riders. William decided to use archers first and then charge up the hill towards the English with mounted knights.

- Who do you think had made the best decisions about how and where to fight?

Now it's your turn

You are going to use sources of evidence about the Battle of Hastings to help you to answer the question: 'Why did William win the Battle of Hastings?'. The pictures are sections of the Bayeux Tapestry. This is an embroidery made on the orders of William's half-brother, Bishop Odo of Bayeux. Bishop Odo fought in the battle, using a club because he was a churchman who was not supposed to kill people. The written sources were by William of Poitiers, personal priest and chronicler to William. A chronicler wrote a record of events. Usually, at this time, the chronicler would be a churchman: hardly anybody else could write. William could not even sign his name!

As you study the battle, decide when luck helped William and when decisions helped him!

Shield wall: a wall of shields held by soldiers standing shoulder to shoulder

Source 1 *Here Norman knights stumble as they charge up the hill towards the English shield wall*

The sound of trumpets showed the start of battle. The English hurled javelins and missiles of all sorts. They made savage blows with their axes. Then the Norman knights rode forward. The English were helped by the advantage of their position on the hill. They stayed there without attempting to advance. The weapons of the English easily cut through shields and other protective armour. Almost the whole of Duke William's front line fell back.

Source 2 *William of Poitiers describes the start of the battle*

* Why were the English doing best at the start of the battle?

Source 3 *Here William lifts his helmet to prove to his men that he is still alive*

The Normans thought that their Duke had fallen, but he rushed after his retreating troops, dragged off his helmet, and showed his bared head. 'Look at me!' he shouted, 'I am still alive! With God's help I shall win'. They took new courage from his words. The Normans realised that they could never overcome the vast army of the English. They therefore pretended to turn and run away. A thousand or more of the English rushed boldly forward. Suddenly the Normans turned their horses and cut off the force which was chasing them. Then they massacred them to the last man. The Normans successfully used this trick twice.

Source 4 *William of Poitiers continues his account of the battle*

- What evidence can you find of luck and decisions helping William?

The end came when Harold, the English king, was killed. The scene from the Bayeux Tapestry shows two figures below the words 'King Harold is killed'. The Bayeux Tapestry seems to show him with an arrow in his eye. One of the written accounts tells us that an arrow that was shot towards the sky struck Harold above the right eye and that it put out one of his eyes. The arrow would have pierced his skull and damaged his brain. Other written sources tell us that after this a Norman knight hacked at his legs. Can you see a man in the tapestry with his legs being hacked?

Source 5
The Death of King Harold

With the death of their king, the English must have realised that their last hope had gone. The king's bodyguard fought on, dying bravely with their fallen king, but the ordinary English soldiers began to give up with exhaustion. They fled from the battlefield, trying to save their own lives.

- Was Godwinson's death caused by luck or William's decisions? Give reasons for your answer.

The Battle of Hastings was over. The Normans had won and William could now claim the right to be King of England.

Now it's your turn

Draw up a grid to show the following:

Godwinson's bad luck	William's good luck	Godwinson's bad decisions	William's good decisions

Check your progress

★ I can describe some of the events in the Battle of Hastings.

★★ I can explain how luck and good decisions helped William to win the battle.

★★★ I can weigh up which was more important in helping William, and give reasons.

Extension work APP

Why did William win the battle of Hastings?

Use the following plan to help answer the question. Refer to your notes on events before the battle and events during the battle. Make sure you include plenty of examples of the different kinds of reasons to make your conclusion convincing.

- Reasons to do with Harold Godwinson's:
  bad luck
  bad decisions

- Reasons to do with William's:
  good luck
  good decisions

Which do you think was more important in explaining why William won the battle, luck or decisions?

Control through castles

William had won a great victory at Hastings but he did not yet control all England. How did he become William the Conqueror?

Getting you thinking

There were about one and a half million English but only about 10,000 Normans to control them.

- What do you think William's main problems were going to be?
- What would you advise him to do?

There were no castles in England before 1066, but the Normans were used to building them as a way of controlling an area. They had a way of building a castle that is known as *motte and bailey*.

- How would the motte and bailey castle help a Norman lord to control the area?

- Why would it be difficult for the English to attack the castle?

Between 1066 and 1087, when William died, the Normans built over 100 castles around the country.

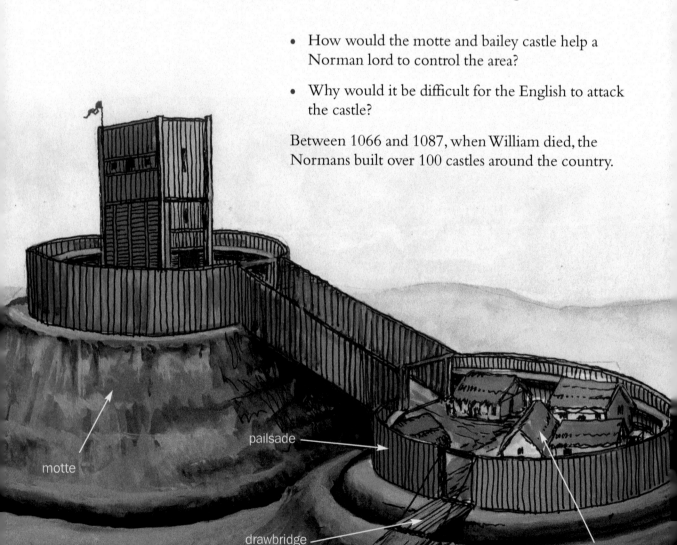

motte

pailsade

drawbridge

bailey

Motte and bailey: This was the type of castle built by the Normans after 1066. The motte was the hill that the castle was built on. The bailey was the area surrounded by the walls.

Where to build the Norman castle?

It was important to choose a good site for a castle. The site had to:

- command a good view over the area
- have a good supply of wood or stones for building
- have water for the moat or, even better, a river to help defend it
- be in a good position to defend
- allow you to get to and from the castle in order to control the area around it
- have a village nearby so the English could be used to do all the hard work building the castle

Now it's your turn

Study the map which shows you five sites where you might build your castle.

In pairs or groups, look at the sites and see how they measure up to the requirements listed above. Decide which site you would build your castle on and why.

Check your progress

I can talk about why William built castles in England.
I can describe some of the features of a motte and bailey castle.
I can talk about how sites for castles were chosen.

Control using terror!

Castles were very useful in helping William to conquer England, but the English could still be troublesome. He needed more methods to control them.

Getting you thinking

King William had invaded England and won the crown, but it did not mean that he had full control of England. Between 1066 and 1070 he was forced to crush many *rebellions*.

This map shows some of the main rebellions that William had to deal with after 1066.

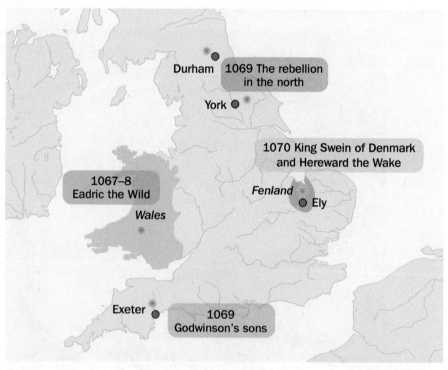

William used terror to crush these rebellions. In 1069 rebels in the north killed the Normans in Durham. They then captured York and were joined by a large Danish army. William marched north, forced the Danes to flee and then destroyed the area. A Norman monk later wrote that corpses lay rotting. In his anger, William ordered that all crops, herds and food of every kind should be burned to ashes. People were left to die of slow starvation. Survivors had to eat cats and dogs. This is called the '*Harrying of the North*'.

- Why do you think that William was so cruel in the way he crushed the northern rebellion?

Rebellion: a violent protest when ordinary people attack the rulers

The story of Hereward the Wake

The most famous rebel was Hereward the Wake. His base was the Isle of Ely, in Eastern England. It was surrounded by rivers and marshes. It would be difficult for the Normans to cross the dangerous marshland to reach Ely.

The first attempt by the Normans failed when the bridge that they built collapsed under the weight of the Norman knights. The Normans then sent a witch to scream curses at the rebels across the marshes. It is said that Hereward was finally defeated after the Normans were shown the secret way across the marshes to the Isle of Ely. Hereward escaped and there are many stories about what happened to him. William cruelly punished some of the rebels. They had their hands or feet cut off. Others had their eyes put out. It was a warning to anybody else who thought about rebelling!

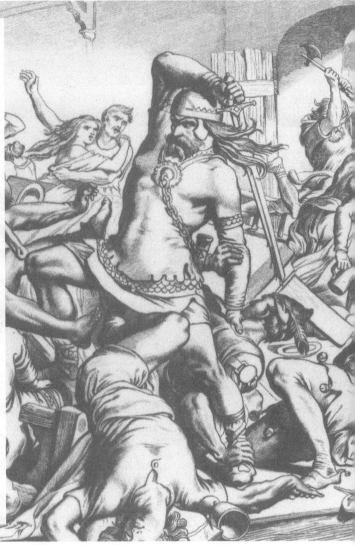

Now it's your turn

How did William use terror tactics to defeat the rebellions?

Extension work

Think about the following questions.

1. Do you think that William was right to use terror?
2. If not, how else should he have gained control of England?

Check your progress

- I can describe how the Normans used terror to stay in power.
- I can talk about the rebellion of Hereward the Wake.
- I can give some reasons why William was so cruel in crushing rebellions.

Harrying of the North: The word 'harry' means to destroy

Controlling land: the feudal system

Objectives

By the end of this lesson you will be able to:

- describe the feudal system
- explain how the feudal system helped William to control England

Castles and terror were useful for controlling England, but William needed a way of ruling every part of England. His method was the *feudal system*.

Getting you thinking

King William had some problems.

He knew that he couldn't be everywhere at once in order to control England.

He knew that the Normans expected to be rewarded. After all, they had risked their lives for him in battle and he wouldn't be king without their help.

- Can you think how he could solve his problems?

There was another danger. If he gave too much land to his barons or allowed them to build too many castles for themselves, they might become too powerful. He had to make sure that they remained loyal and helped him to control England. He especially wanted them to provide knights for his army.

The answer was the *feudal system*.

LAND **SERVICE**

The king
Owner of all the land
Kept about a quarter for his own use and gave the rest to his tenants-in-chief. This was usually spread out around the country.

Tenants-in-Chief
About 200
Mainly barons and bishops

Under-tenants
About 4,000
Mainly knights

Peasants
About 1,500,000
Villeins (richer peasants)
Bordars and cottars (poorer peasants)

Feudal system: a system of giving out land in return for services and loyalty

At each level of the feudal system the lord kept land for his own use. This would be farmed by the English peasants. A lord would build a castle to control his land.

Some land was given to the next level of society by the lord.

In return for the grant of land from a lord, each level had to:
- swear to be loyal to their lord; this was called doing homage
- swear to provide service for their lord

What service did each level have to provide for their lord?
- A peasant's main service was to work on his lord's land for an agreed number of days each week.
- A knight's service was to fight for his lord.
- A *tenant*-in-chief's main service was to provide an agreed number of knights for the king for up to 40 days a year.
- There were also taxes and rents that had to be paid to the lord.

Now it's your turn

Look carefully at the picture on the right.

Can you explain what is happening in the picture?

Check your progress

★ I can talk about who was given land in the feudal system, and what they had to give back in return.

★★ I can explain how people below the king benefited from the feudal system.

★★★ I can explain how the system helped the king to stay in power.

Tenant: a person who received land in return for services and loyalty

Control by a book

By the end of his reign King William had gained control of most of England. Next you will find out about how he made sure he knew all about his kingdom. In the winter of 1085–86, he ordered something very unusual to be carried out. Nothing like it had ever been done before!

Objectives

By the end of this lesson you will be able to:

- explain the reasons why the Domesday survey was carried out

- explain how the information recorded in the Domesday Book helped William and future rulers to control England

Getting you thinking

Today, the government carries out a *census* every ten years.
- Do you know what kinds of questions are asked?
- Why do you think that it is carried out?

The very first census took place under King William.

Read the following extract.

> At Gloucester at midwinter the King had deep speech with his counsellors and sent men all over England to each shire to find out who owned the land, how much each landowner held in land and livestock, and what it was worth.
>
> *Extract from The Anglo-Saxon Chronicle for 1085*

Census: a survey carried out every ten years about the people living in this country

An official called a commissioner was to ask the questions. Normally, six villagers and the reeve (foreman) would be asked. All of the answers were double-checked in a second visit! The officials visited over 13,000 places. It took them over a year to carry out the visits. All the information was sent to Winchester where a monk wrote up the answers. The people called it the Domesday Book. The word Domesday means 'God's Judgement Day'. The people were being judged so that the king could claim his taxes!

Below is a section taken from the area around Ripon in North Yorkshire. It has been written in English, but the original book was in Latin.

Land of the Archbishop of York

In Ripon 10 ploughs are possible. Archbishop Aldred held this land before 1066. Now Archbishop Thomas is the lord of the manor. There is one mill 10 shillings (50 pence) and one fishery 3 shillings (15 pence). To this manor there belong other villages in which 30 ploughs are possible. All this land is waste, except for the village of Markington.

Now it's your turn

How did William use the Domesday Book to help him control England?

Think about:
- what information the king learned from it
- how we can tell from the survey that the Normans had gained control over England

Check your progress

I can describe what the Domesday Survey was.
I can explain what information the Normans wanted to find out.
I can explain how the Domesday Book helped the Normans to control England.

Domesday Book: a report on all the land and wealth of England put together by William in 1086–87

What problems did monarchs face after 1066?

Objectives

By the end of this lesson you will be able to:

- describe problems and challenges that monarchs had to face after William
- explain how the problems challenged the monarchs' power

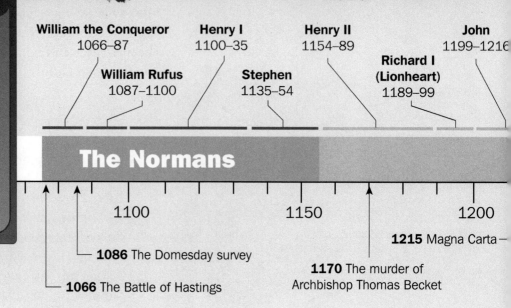

William the Conqueror 1066–87

William Rufus 1087–1100

Henry I 1100–35

Stephen 1135–54

Henry II 1154–89

Richard I (Lionheart) 1189–99

John 1199–1216

The Normans

1100   1150   1200

1215 Magna Carta

1086 The Domesday survey

1170 The murder of Archbishop Thomas Becket

1066 The Battle of Hastings

Getting you thinking

William the Conqueror seemed to have got a firm control over the country by 1087. But monarchs still faced all sorts of challenges to their control.

- What kinds of challenges do you think that monarchs would still face?
- Can you see any examples in the timeline?

Some problems are described below.

Succession

The word 'succession' means who had the right to become the next ruler. Can you remember the problem at the start of 1066? The Norman Conquest didn't end this problem. In 1100, Henry I had his older brother, William Rufus, killed in a hunting 'accident' in the New Forest. When Henry himself died, he left only a daughter. Even though he had made the barons take an oath to recognise Matilda, many of them supported his nephew, Stephen. *Civil war* broke out in England.

Succession: the way the right to rule is passed on to the next in line

Rebellions by the barons

The barons would take any chance to get more power from a weak king. John and Henry III both faced rebellions by their barons.

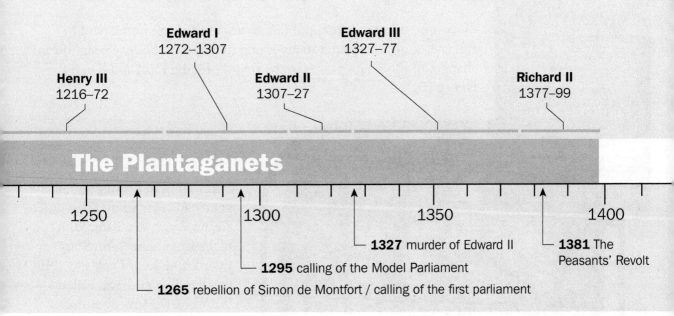

Edward I
1272–1307

Edward III
1327–77

Henry III
1216–72

Edward II
1307–27

Richard II
1377–99

The Plantaganets

1250   1300   1350   1400

1327 murder of Edward II

1381 The Peasants' Revolt

1295 calling of the Model Parliament

1265 rebellion of Simon de Montfort / calling of the first parliament

The church

Many kings clashed with the church about rights. The church was a powerful landowner with a strong influence over people's beliefs. Its head was the Pope in Rome. King Henry II's quarrel with the Archbishop, Thomas Becket, led to Becket's murder inside Canterbury Cathedral. When King John quarrelled with the church, it went on strike for five years.

The Peasants' Revolt, 1381

In 1381, the peasants of Kent and Essex marched on London, stormed the Tower of London and murdered some of the king's main officials, including the Lord Treasurer.

Now it's your turn APP

Which do you think was the greatest problem for monarchs in the Middle Ages?

Check your progress

I can talk about some of the problems facing monarchs after 1066.

I can talk about the different groups who might have threatened the monarch's power.

I can use the timeline to connect events to the rule of different kings.

King John and the development of royal power

Over time things change, and the power of the king in the Middle Ages certainly changed. You are going to find out about two significant changes in the king's power in the reigns of King John and King Henry III.

Getting you thinking

Sometimes in history people get a bad reputation. They don't always deserve it. King John's nicknames were 'John Soft-sword' and 'John Lackland'. His brother, Richard, was called 'Lionheart'. How does this compare?

A monk called Matthew Paris wrote that:

> John was a wicked ruler who did not behave like a king. He was greedy and took as much money as he could from his people. Hell is too good for a horrible person like him.

King John kneeling in prayer

In the Middle Ages, the barons and church expected that a king would:
- be a good warrior
- involve the barons in the running of the country and treat them with respect
- support the church and recognise its rights

Look at the statements below and try to work out if King John's reputation was deserved. Do they show that John was a good or a bad king?
- John gave top jobs to foreigners, not barons.
- John tried to make the barons pay extra taxes, for example when a son inherited his father's lands. John needed the taxes to pay for his war with France.
- John won battles against Wales, Scotland and Ireland.
- John lost wars against France. In 1204 the French captured Normandy.
- In 1214 a war began between John and his barons.
- John argued with the Pope, who ordered all the priests to go on strike. For five years the churches were closed so that there were no baptisms or funerals. People were worried that they would go to hell.
- John tried hard to be a good king. He visited all parts of England and helped poor people, including widows and orphans.
- He ordered that Jews were not to be harmed in any way. Can you think why this did not win the support of the barons or the church?

Now it's your turn

Write a report on whether you think King John deserves the reputation Matthew Paris gave him.

Make sure that you include:
- reasons why John was seen as a bad king
- reasons why John might be seen as a good king

Check your progress

I can give reasons why King John had such a bad reputation.
I can talk about what was expected of a king in the Middle Ages and why John failed to match up.
I can decide whether John deserves his bad reputation, and give reasons.

The Magna Carta

Objectives

By the end of this lesson you will be able to:

- describe what the Magna Carta was
- decide how important you think the Magna Carta was

King John did not do what his barons expected of him. Now you are going to find out how this affected his power.

Getting you thinking

Everybody has *human rights* set out in the law.

- What do you think this means?
- Why do you think it is important to have rights?
- Do you know any of your rights?

The most famous *charter* of rights in English history is Magna Carta. The barons forced King John to agree to it in 1215. It set out the rights of all the *freemen* in the country. How important was this?

Clause 1: The king must not interfere with the church.

Clause 2: When a baron inherits land he should pay the king no more than £100.

Clause 12: The king must not collect any new taxes without the agreement of the barons and bishops.

Clause 39: No freeman to be put in prison without a proper trial **by a jury.**

Clause 40: The king's judges should be fair to everybody and justice should be given without delay or bribes.

Clause 42: Everybody should be free to enter or leave the country.

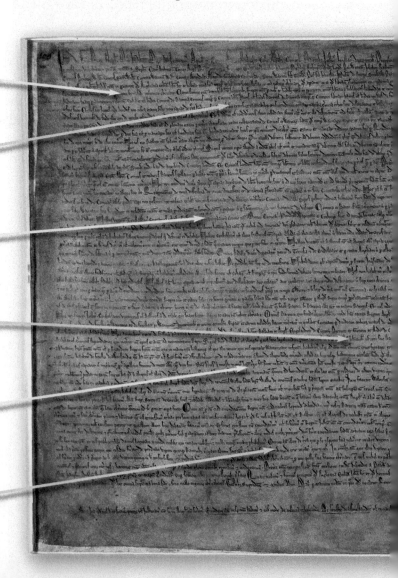

Charter: a written grant of rights by a king or queen
Human rights: fair treatment for all

Now it's your turn

So how important do you think that Magna Carta was?

Below are some facts about Magna Carta to help you decide. For each point explain why you think this makes Magna Carta more or less important. Give each one a score out of 10, where 10 means very important.

- Much of the *Magna Carta* was copied from the Charter of Liberties agreed in 1100 by Henry I.
- It was agreed to by every English king for hundreds of years and used as a guarantee of rights throughout the Middle Ages.
- Many of the points in the charter were meant to protect the rights of the barons and bishops rather than the ordinary people.
- Some of Magna Carta's points still apply today. The main one is the right to a trial without delay. We call this the right of habeas corpus.
- It was the first time that a document of rights had been forced on to an English king by his subjects to protect their rights.

Check your progress

★ I can say what the Magna Carta was.

★★ I can describe some of the rights it set out.

★★★ I can explain why people think it is such an important document in English history.

Freemen: people who were free in law and did not 'belong' to a lord
Magna Carta: Latin words meaning 'Great Charter'

The beginnings of parliament

The second important change in the king's power came in the reign of King John's son, King Henry III.

Getting you thinking

You will probably have heard of parliament but:
- Do you know what it does?
- Do you know which two parts (or houses) make up parliament?

In this section we are going to find out how Parliament began.

Kings have always had councils of powerful subjects to advise them on how to run the country. The Anglo-Saxon *Witan* was made up of nobles and bishops. Norman kings met with their Great Council made up of the tenants-in-chief, the Norman barons and bishops.

The most important development came because of a rebellion against the king by a baron called Simon de Montfort.

Rebellion!

The Magna Carta said that the king must speak to his Great Council before changing taxes. King John's son, Henry III, argued with his barons about taxes. A war broke out between the king and Simon de Montfort, the leader of the barons. De Montfort defeated the king's army at the battle of Lewes in 1264. He was the most powerful man in England but other barons soon became jealous of him. De Montfort decided that he needed more support.

For the next Great Council meeting in 1265, de Montfort invited some new members. As well as the barons and bishops (the Lords), he invited two *knights* from every county and two rich men, known as *burgesses*, from every town that was friendly to him. By 1265, towns were growing richer and the merchants wanted a say in running the country in return for their taxes. These were members of the common people, or Commons. The new members were *elected*.

Burgesses: mostly rich merchants in the towns.
Elected: voted for   *Witan: the Anglo-Saxon council to the king*

Soon afterwards, de Montfort was killed in battle by Henry III's son, Edward. It looked as if the Council would go back to its old ways, but the idea of inviting the Commons to the Great Council did not die with Simon de Montfort.

Soon, people began to use the name '*parliament*' for this new council. It comes from the French word 'parler' which means 'to speak'.

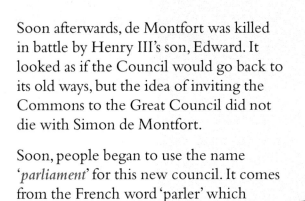

Simon de Montfort, the leader of the barons

Now it's your turn

Write a short explanation for a history magazine about how parliament began. You can use up to 100 words.

Check your progress

★ I can talk about how parliament began.
★★ I can describe how kings were advised before Simon de Montfort's rebellion.
★★★ I can name some of the different groups who were invited to parliament and who was left out.

Knights: *By 1265 this meant the wealthy landowners of the counties*
Parliament: *a meeting of Lords and Commons to advise the king*

Parliament develops during the Middle Ages

Objectives

By the end of this lesson you will be able to:

- explain how parliament developed during the Middle Ages

- explain how it has changed and stayed the same since 1295

The king's power had changed and so did parliament's. You are going to see how parliament's powers changed in the Middle Ages.

Getting you thinking

Have you ever heard somebody called a 'model student'? What do you think the word 'model' means when it is used in this way?

In 1295 King Edward I called a parliament which became known as the Model Parliament. Why do you think that it was called this?

King Edward I and his Model Parliament. Edward is on the throne, surrounded by his Lords and Commons

The Model Parliament

In 1295 Edward I needed money for a war. He copied Simon de Montfort's idea and called a parliament made up of the monarch (himself), the Lords (barons and bishops) and the Commons (knights from the counties and burgesses from the towns).

- Why do you think he called the Commons if the idea had begun in a rebellion against his father?

This parliament became known as the *Model Parliament* because it has been the model for parliaments ever since. In return for voting him taxes to pay for his war, Edward allowed it to pass some laws. These have remained parliament's two main jobs: voting on taxes and passing new laws.

How parliament has changed

The Model Parliament 1295	Parliament today
The king sat in parliament and was in charge of the government.	The monarch is only allowed in parliament when invited. The head of the government is the prime minister.
The Lords and Commons sat together.	The Lords and Commons have been separate since the 1300s.
The Lords had more power than the Commons.	The House of Commons has most power. The House of Lords cannot stop the Commons getting a new law and the monarch agrees to what parliament wants.
Only wealthy men could elect members of the Commons.	Almost all adults are able to vote.
Parliament was called and was ended when the king wanted.	A new parliament has to be elected at least every five years. There must always be a parliament.

Now it's your turn

Write your next entry for history magazine. This one is about 'How parliament has changed and stayed the same since The Model Parliament of 1295'.

Use the picture and the information to write your report. Remember, you are only allowed 100 words!

Check your progress

I can describe what the Lords and the Commons are.

I can explain what the Model Parliament was.

I can describe some of the ways that parliament has changed and stayed the same since the Model Parliament.

Women in the Middle Ages: Matilda

Objectives

By the end of this lesson you will be able to:

- explain the reasons why Matilda was such an important person in the 12th century

Getting you thinking

On Matilda's gravestone is written:

> 'Here lies Matilda, the daughter, wife and mother of Henry.'

Can you work out how this might make sense?

Matilda was the daughter of King Henry I. Her first husband was the Emperor Henry V of Germany and her son was King Henry II. However, Matilda was never Queen of England. Read below to find out why.

Matilda, the 'Lady of the English'

The royal bride

In the Middle Ages a female was just as important as a male when it came to making a family powerful. Why do you think this was?

At the age of 7, Matilda was promised in marriage to the German emperor, Henry V. She married him when she was 12 and was widowed at 23. When she was 26 she was married to Count Geoffrey of Anjou, who was 15. Matilda had three sons. Her eldest became King Henry II of England in 1154.

Matilda at war

Matilda's brother, William, drowned in 1120. Matilda was now the only *legitimate heir* to the throne. Her Father, King Henry I, made the Anglo-Norman barons take an oath to accept Matilda as his heir. But when Henry I died many of them supported her cousin, Stephen. Civil war broke out.

Why do you think that the barons supported Stephen despite their oath to support Matilda?

Matilda invaded England to claim the throne from Stephen. At the battle of Lincoln 1141, Matilda defeated and captured Stephen but let him go in return for her half-brother who had also been captured.

Lady of the English

Matilda refused to be crowned as queen. She said that all previous queens had the title because they were married to a king. She would be known as 'The Lady of the English'. Soon afterwards the Londoners rebelled against Matilda. She was forced to flee and Stephen became king.

Matilda's heir

In 1153, Stephen's son died. Stephen recognised Matilda's son, Henry, as his heir. Matilda never ruled England as queen but her son became king. Matilda retired to live in Rouen, Normandy, where she is buried.

Now it's your turn

On Matilda's grave is written:

'Great by Birth, Greater by Marriage, Greatest in her Offspring. Here lies Matilda, the daughter, wife and mother of Henry.'

Use this and the information above to write about the life of Matilda and why she was so important.

Check your progress

- I can describe some of the things that happened to Matilda in her life.
- I can explain the lines written on Matilda's grave.
- I can explain why Matilda was such an important figure in the 12th century.

Legitimate heir: a child of the king and queen who could by law become the next ruler

Eleanor of Aquitaine

Objectives

By the end of this lesson you will be able to:

- describe some of the events of Eleanor of Aquitaine's life
- explain why Eleanor of Aquitaine's life was so remarkable

A woman with an even more extraordinary story than that of Matilda was Eleanor of Aquitaine, Matilda's daughter-in-law.

Getting you thinking

- Can you think what kinds of behaviour might have seemed unusual for a princess in the 12th century?

Eleanor of Aquitaine was one of the wealthiest and most powerful women in western Europe. Her exciting life showed that she was definitely not prepared to be a typical royal wife or mother!

Eleanor and her first husband, King Louis VII of France

1 Aged 15, Eleanor became ruler of Aquitaine. Eleanor was well educated, not just in the normal female subjects, but also in riding, hawking and hunting. She had all the qualities a king would look for in a wife, including beauty. But she was also a strong-willed and intelligent woman.

England

London

Normandy

Paris

Anjou   France

Poitiers

Bordeaux

Aquitaine

Mediterrane Sea

Spain

Now it's your turn

As you read about Eleanor's life, note all the remarkable things about her.

Now it's your turn APP

'The adventures of Eleanor, the most exciting woman in the Middle Ages!'
Now write the story that goes with this heading.

2 Her guardian, Louis the Fat, king of France, couldn't wait to marry Eleanor to his son. Just days after the wedding, her husband became King Louis VII of France. He was madly in love with Eleanor, but he was not her idea of a suitable husband.

3 After a quarrel with the church, for which Eleanor was blamed, Louis decided to go on crusade to the Holy Land. Eleanor went with him. She soon fell out with her husband and he even put her in prison. Eleanor decided she had put up with Louis long enough! After they got back from the crusade the church annulled (cancelled) the marriage.

Germany (Holy Roman Empire)

4 Eleanor sent a messenger to Henry, Matilda's son, to come and marry her! The wedding took place six weeks later. She was thirty and he was nineteen. Soon Henry became King Henry II of England. Their marriage created a great empire, from the borders of Scotland to the Pyrenees. It was a stormy marriage between two strong characters, but Eleanor bore eight children, including two future kings. When she supported a rebellion by three of the sons against Henry, her husband had her imprisoned for sixteen years!

Austria

5 Eleanor was freed by Richard, her favourite son, when Henry II died. The adventures did not stop in her old age. She ruled England when Richard went on crusade. When he was captured, she organised the ransom and went to Austria to fetch him. Aged nearly 80, she crossed the Pyrenees to escort her granddaughter, Blanche of Castille. By the time of her death in 1204 Eleanor had survived all except two of her children.

Antioch ●

Check your progress

I can talk about who Eleanor of Aquitaine was.
I can describe some of her adventures.
I can give reasons why Eleanor is thought to be a significant figure in history.

Palestine

Jerusalem ●

How do we know the church was powerful in the Middle Ages?

Objectives

By the end of this unit you will be able to:

- describe the power of the church in the Middle Ages
- explain some reasons why the church had a powerful influence in the Middle Ages

Getting you thinking

This picture is an aerial view of Richmond in Yorkshire. Look for the castle and the church near it. They were the largest buildings in Richmond in the Middle Ages. What does this tell us about who had power? *Medieval* people understood who had power. They knew that they must obey the lord in the castle who represented the power of the king, and the priest in the church who represented the power of the church. At this time 'church' meant the Catholic Church, the only church in western Europe.

The diagram below shows the organisation of the church.
- In what ways is the organisation similar to the feudal system?
- In what ways is it different?

The secular clergy who worked among the ordinary people (laity).

The regular clergy who did not mix with ordinary people, but lived apart from them.

Pope
Head of the church

Cardinals
When a pope died, they chose the new pope

Archbishops
Responsible for church matters in a large area, based at a cathedral

Abbots and abbesses
Heads of large monasteries and nunneries

Bishops
Responsible for part of the Archbishop's land. Based at a cathedral

Priors and prioresses
Heads of smaller monasteries and nunneries

Parish priests
Looked after the beliefs of ordinary people in part of the bishop's land

Monks, friars and nuns
Chose to live in monasteries or nunneries

Non-ordained clergy
Did jobs such as collecting church tax

Lay brothers
Monks' servants

The king and the church worked together to show their power over the ordinary people. The king gained authority after he had been crowned by an archbishop or bishop. Archbishops, bishops and abbots were often tenants-in-chief of the king. In addition to being important in the church they took part in governing England.

The priest was often the only person in a village or town who could read. He might also be able to write. Kings had to rely on priests to keep government records and help them run the country.

Now it's your turn

1 Make a list of all the reasons the church was powerful in the Middle Ages.
2 Give one piece of evidence to support each of your reasons.
3 Do you think the king or the church was more powerful? Explain the reasons for your answer.

Check your progress

I can say who people in the Middle Ages had to obey.
I can talk about how the church was organised.
I can talk about how the king and the church worked together to run the country.

How did the church make people obey its rules?

Objectives

By the end of this lesson you will be able to:

- describe what medieval people thought hell was like
- explain how the church used fear to control people

You have found out that the church had wealth, power and a clear organisation. People in the Middle Ages must have been impressed by this and the large churches and cathedrals they saw, but why did they behave in the way they were told to by the priests?

A medieval painting of hell

Heaven: where the souls of good people went after purgatory
Hell: where the souls of bad people went

Getting you thinking

How do you know what is right and wrong? Why do you obey rules?

In the Middle Ages the church gave people strict guidelines about how to live their lives. Of course they did not always obey the rules, but the church made sure they knew the consequences if they broke the rules.

Pictures like this were painted on the wall above the door of the parish church. People saw them on their way out of church. It reminded them what would happen when they died if they lived a bad life. The priest reminded them too. He told them about how their souls would be tortured for their sins after they died.

The priest told them that when they died a judgement would be made. The judgement was made on the day of *doom*. This was the day at the end of the world, when everyone would be judged by God and a decision made about what would happen to their soul. If the judgement was that they had committed serious sins their soul would go to *hell* and be tortured for ever.

If the person had been mostly good their soul would go to *heaven* in the end. In heaven souls would have no worries. They would spend their time worshipping God. But no-one was totally good. To make up for any sins, souls would go to *purgatory* for years. In purgatory they would be tortured until all their sins were washed away. Then they would go to heaven.

Now it's your turn

1 Describe what the picture shows. Why do you think the souls are shown as people with no clothes?
2 Why do you think pictures like this one were painted on the walls of churches?
3 Why did the church make hell seem so frightening?
4 Do you think people thought it was easy or difficult to get to heaven? Use the picture to give you clues.
5 What did people hope would happen to them when they died?

Check your progress

I can talk about the meaning of heaven, hell and purgatory.
I can describe why medieval people feared hell and purgatory.
I can explain why medieval people tried to do good deeds.

Doom: judgement for sinners
Purgatory: where the souls of good people went for years, to make up for their sins

How did the church give people hope?

You have seen how the church made people frightened of hell, but the church also gave people hope that they could get to heaven. You are going to find out how it did this.

Getting you thinking

Do you work better if you are threatened with a punishment if you do badly or if you are shown how to do well? Most people need a reward for doing well and medieval people were no different.

How to get to heaven

Medieval people feared hell, but they needed to be shown how to get to heaven. Look at this picture. This window is in a church in York. The picture in the glass was easy for medieval people to see and understand. The window shows the six good deeds that Jesus said people should do if they wanted to go to heaven. The priest would tell them about these good deeds too. Can you see what the six good deeds are?

Pilgrimage: a journey to a holy place such as Jerusalem
Pardoner: a man who sells 'pardons'

Besides doing good deeds, people believed the saints could help them reduce the number of years they would spend in purgatory. Getting close to saints by visiting their graves or paying to see objects that had belonged to them would help. This extract is from a medieval story about people going on a *pilgrimage*. It gives us more ideas that people had about ways of getting to heaven. How many can you find?

> … folks long to go on pilgrimages,
> To distant saints, known in sundry lands
> And specially, from every shire's end
> Of England, to Canterbury they wend [go],
> The holy blissful martyr for to seek …
> With them rode a gentle Pardoner …
> A Christ's image hung upon his cap.
> His wallet lay open on his lap,
> Brimful of pardons come from Rome all hot…
> In his bag he had a pillow there,
> Which that he said, was Our Lady's veil.

Now it's your turn

1 Make a list of all the ways people helped themselves to get to heaven.

2 For each one, write down whether it was easy or difficult for medieval people to do.

Check your progress

★ I can describe some things medieval people did to try to get to heaven.

★★ I can talk about things people did to try to reduce their time in purgatory.

★★★ I can talk about what gave people hope that they might go to heaven.

Pardon: a certificate reducing the number of years in purgatory
Our Lady: Mary, the mother of Jesus

How did the church control knowledge?

Objectives

By the end of this lesson you will be able to:

- explain how the church controlled knowledge
- explain the effects of the church's control of knowledge

So far you have seen how church beliefs made people behave well. Now you will find out how the church had power over knowledge.

Getting you thinking

Where do you look when you want to find out something? On the internet? In a reference book? Can you look up whatever you want to? What prevents you?

In the Middle Ages there were many problems in gaining knowledge. There was no internet. Books were hand written in Latin. They were rare and most of them were in monastery libraries, where they were chained up to stop them being stolen, like the ones in the photograph. Schools and universities were controlled by the church. This made it difficult for anyone who wanted to challenge the church's ideas to speak out.

Many of the books were about religious ideas, but some were about science and medicine. The books were often based on Ancient Greek and Roman books. Over the years mistakes had been made in copying them. Very little research was done to test scientific ideas. The church taught people that when they died their body should be buried, ready for Judgement Day. No-one wanted to allow trainee doctors to learn by cutting up their dead body!

Glass cutters were beginning to make reading glasses. We know this because there are pictures of medieval people wearing glasses. However, lenses were not yet good enough to make microscopes for studying parts of the body in detail. Germs are too small to see without a microscope. No wonder medical knowledge was very basic!

Monks did, however, make a big contribution to treating disease. They had useful books about how herbs can be used to treat illnesses. Some monks were experts in growing herbs and making useful medicines.

The Chained Library
at Hereford Cathedral

Medieval maps tell
us what people thought the
world was like. You may have heard that
people thought the earth was flat. We now know
this isn't true. The church did teach, though, that the earth
was at the centre of the universe. Any medieval person who
contradicted the church was in danger of being called a *heretic*. Heretics
were burned at the stake to make them suffer the pains of hell on earth.

Now it's your turn

Use what you have read to decide which of
these ideas would be thought of as heresy.
Explain your answers.
- The earth is a sphere.
- The earth goes round the sun.
- It is a good idea to dissect dead bodies.
- Books should be available for anyone to read.
- Everyone should be able to read.

Check your progress

- I can talk about who
  controlled knowledge in the
  Middle Ages.
- I can explain why the
  church wanted to control
  knowledge.
- I can describe some effects
  of the church's control of
  knowledge.

Heretic: a person who challenges the beliefs and ideas of the church

Why did so many people become monks and nuns?

Objectives

By the end of this lesson you will be able to:

- describe what monks and nuns did

- explain why many people wanted to be monks in the Middle Ages

It may seem strange to us that there were so many monasteries and nunneries where people shut themselves away from everyday life and prayed. Why do you think they did this?

Getting you thinking

What do you want to do when you leave school? You have so much choice!

Medieval people had little choice. They did the same jobs their parents did.

The remains of Jervaulx Abbey, a former monastery in North Yorkshire

Medieval people could become a monk or a nun. A boy might go to a monastery school. He would learn to read and write – in Latin, of course. Next, he would spend time living in a monastery, deciding if this was the life for him. Each day he would go to many church services. Besides this he would spend time on book work and do some practical work. He would eat a vegetarian diet, with one or two meals a day, depending on the time of year. If he decided to join the monastery for life, he would make three promises: to live like a poor person, avoid sexual relationships and obey the *abbot*.

- Does this appeal to you? What were the good points for medieval people?

Monasteries often controlled large areas of land. There was work to be done managing the farms, often with sheep on them. A monk might become a chronicler, recording events year by year. He could become an expert in herbal medicine or in writing and illustrating books. He could study science or astronomy. Nuns also did skilled work, doing embroidery rather than copying books.

Do you still think it's a bad job? Then think of the options. If you were the eldest son of a lord you would be fine. You would inherit his lands. But what if you were a younger son? There were few choices. What if you were a girl? You would get married. Then you would have children, a dangerous process in medieval times. Many of the babies would die young. Does becoming a monk or nun sound any better now?

Now it's your turn

Weigh up the good and bad points about becoming a monk or nun.
1 Draw a pair of weighing scales.
2 On one side put the good points about being a monk or nun.
3 On the other put the bad points .
4 Give each point a score from 1–5 (5 is good, 1 is bad)

Remember to think about it from a medieval person's point of view.

What is your conclusion? Do you understand why so many medieval people joined monasteries and nunneries?

Check your progress

I can describe the work done by monks and nuns.
I can explain the good and bad points of being a monk or nun.
I can understand the reasons medieval people became monks or nuns.

Abbot: the monk in charge of a monastery or abbey

How popular was the church at the end of the Middle Ages?

Objectives

By the end of this lesson you will be able to:

- use sources to describe the strengths and problems of the church by 1500

- use your knowledge about the church to explain why historians have different views about how popular the church was by 1500

You have probably decided that people were more religious in the Middle Ages than they are in Britain today. Now you will investigate how popular the church was by 1500.

Getting you thinking

These two extracts show what two historians wrote about the popularity of the church at the end of the Middle Ages:

> 'The churchmen's power and influence in society was more apparent than real.'
> (A.G.Dickens)

> 'There is little sign of growing popular *hostility* towards Catholicism.'
> (J.J.Scarisbrick)

Discuss with a partner what the historians mean. Does it seem strange that historians have different opinions? Look carefully at all the sources and see why you think there are different views.

Source 1 *An English parish church from the end of the Middle Ages. Rich people in the village paid for the church to be enlarged*

Hostility: bad feeling

Now it's your turn

- Look carefully at these sources. What do they tell you about the popularity of the church at the end of the Middle Ages? As you look at them, decide if they support Dickens's view or Scarisbrick's view.

Jesus Christ was a poor man from his birth to his death, avoiding worldly riches. The Pope at Rome, in contrast, from the time of his birth until he dies, tries to be worldly rich. Bishops and priests should not tax the poor people, for this is worse than common robbery.

Source 2 *From the writings of John Wycliff (1320–1384). His ideas influenced a group of heretics called Lollards*

Many false persons do wickedly preach and teach new ideas against the holy Catholic Church. They stir up rebellion. From now on no-one shall preach without a licence from the bishop. Any persons going against the law shall be burnt before the people in a public place.

Source 3 *From a law against heretics, passed by parliament in 1401*

People always go to church on Sunday and give generously to the church and the poor. There is not a parish church in the kingdom that does not have crucifixes, candlesticks and silver cups, as well as many other ornaments worthy of a cathedral.

Source 4 *An Italian visitor's description written in 1497*

- What have you decided? Can you suggest why the historians have different views?

Now it's your turn

You are a churchman on a mission to England from Rome. Your task is to write a report for the Pope about the church in England. He wants to know how popular the church is.

Check your progress

I can talk about the difference between the two historians' views.
I can describe the two different views about the church.
I can suggest reasons why the historians have different views.

A struggle for power: Henry II and Thomas Becket

Objectives

By the end of this lesson you will be able to:

- explain the reasons why Henry II and Thomas Becket fell out with each other
- explain the reasons why Thomas Becket was murdered at Canterbury Cathedral in 1170

You have found out that there were two powerful organisations in England, the king's government and the church. They both had great power, but which was more powerful? Which one would win when they quarrelled?

Getting you thinking

- Have you ever fallen out with a friend?
- Did you manage to make friends again?

Thomas Becket in front of King Henry II

The story of Henry II and Thomas Becket

When Henry II was king he tried to get more power over the church. When churchmen broke the law, they were given special privileges. They had the right to be tried in a church law court instead of the king's law court. They were given lighter punishments. Henry II wanted them to be under his power in the king's law courts. To get his own way, Henry II gave his friend Thomas Becket the top job in the church in England: Archbishop of Canterbury. However, Henry's plan did not work out as expected. Becket took the church's side. He and Henry fell out. They were now enemies instead of friends.

Now it's your turn

As you read about how the quarrel developed, decide who was more to blame: Henry or Becket.

- Becket was Henry II's Chancellor (chief government official) for eight years. He always supported Henry II against the church.
- In 1161 Becket was chosen as Archbishop of Canterbury: he immediately resigned as Chancellor and took the church's side against Henry II.
- Becket refused to allow clergymen who broke the king's law to be tried in the king's law courts.
- Henry decided to have his eldest son crowned to make sure he was the next king. The Archbishop of York carried out the coronation. This was an insult to Becket.
- Becket was angry because he should have carried out this action. He excommunicated the bishops involved in the coronation.

The quarrel between Henry and Becket ended in 1170. On Christmas Day Henry flew into a violent rage when he heard that Becket had defied him yet again. We don't know exactly what the king said, but four knights who heard him thought that Henry wanted Becket dead. They travelled to Canterbury and on 29 December 1170 they murdered Becket in his cathedral.

Who do you think was most to blame for the murder? Was it Henry II who had lost his temper? Was it Becket who had provoked Henry? Was it the knights who did what they thought Henry wanted?

Check your progress

I can describe what the quarrel between Henry II and Becket was about.
I can talk about how the quarrel led to Becket's death.
I can decide who was to blame for Becket's death, and give evidence.

Objectives

By the end of this lesson you will be able to:

- explain the results of an event
- reach a judgement based on evidence

Becket had been murdered, but had Henry really won the power struggle between himself and the church?

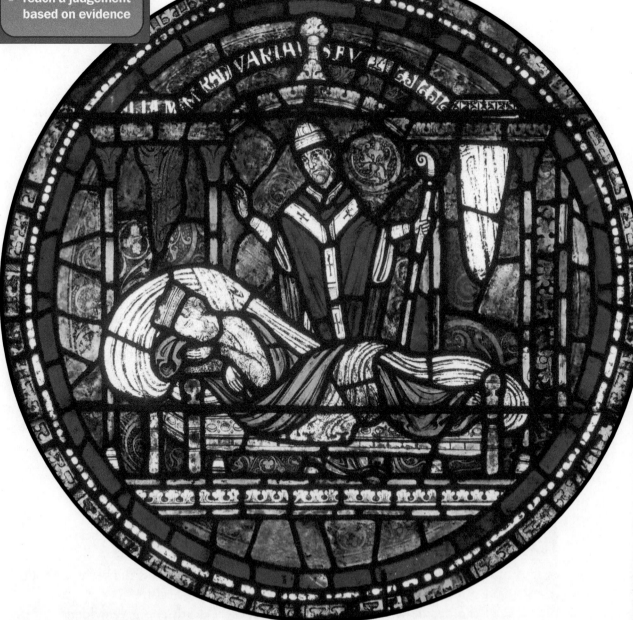

A stained glass window in Canterbury Cathedral showing Henry and Becket

Crusade: a holy war to conquer Jerusalem   *Martyr: a person who is killed for their beliefs*
Jerusalem: a city that is holy for Jews, Christians and Muslims

Getting you thinking

Read this account of what King Henry II did in 1174:

1 Why do you think Henry behaved in this way?

2 Was he feeling guilty?

3 What had he done to deserve such a severe punishment?

> After a short time King Henry made a hasty journey across England. When he reached Canterbury he leapt off his horse and, putting aside his royal dignity, he assumed the appearance of a pilgrim and went to the cathedral. There, with streaming tears, groans and sighs, he made his way to the glorious *martyr*'s [Becket's] tomb. Lying flat on his face with his arms outstretched, he remained there for a long time in prayer. He subjected himself to harsh discipline from cuts with rods, receiving three or even five strokes from each of the monks in turn, of whom a large number had gathered.
>
> **Source 1** *from a medieval account of the story of Thomas Becket*

Now it's your turn

Look at this list of events that happened after the murder of Becket.

Do you think the king or the church won the quarrel in the end?

There is evidence for both sides, so make sure you give evidence to support your judgement.

Immediately after Becket's murder King Henry sent messengers to the Pope to plead his innocence, but the Pope refused to see them.

The Pope *excommunicated* the murderers of Becket and anyone who had suggested the deed or helped them.

- In 1173 Pope Alexander III declared that Becket was a saint.
- Pope Alexander III forgave King Henry for any part he had played in the murder of Becket.
- King Henry promised to give money to the church each year, enough to pay for 200 knights to defend the land of *Jerusalem*.
- King Henry promised to go on a *crusade*, but he did not do so.
- In 1174 King Henry was beaten at Thomas Becket's tomb.
- King Henry gave land to some monasteries and made sure they were strictly run. He also founded two hospitals for *lepers*.

Check your progress

I can talk about what happened after Becket's death.
I can talk about what Henry did, and why he might have behaved that way.
I can decide who won the quarrel between Henry and Becket, and give reasons.

Leper: a person who suffers from an infectious blood disease called leprosy
Excommunicated: expelled from the church

What was so important about Jerusalem?

So far you have found out about what rulers did in England. Now you are going to compare England with the Muslim empire of the Middle East. The two cultures met in a series of wars known as the crusades. In between the wars, the English found they had much to learn from the Muslims.

Getting you thinking

There are many areas of the world today where wars and conflict are influenced by religion. Below you can see a picture of forces involved in the conflict in Afghanistan which began in 2001. Where in the world are wars happening today?

Pilgrimage: *a journey made for religious reasons*
Crusades: *a series of wars between Christians and Muslims*

In the Middle Ages, Christians and Muslims fought religious wars for almost 200 years. These wars are known as the crusades.

This picture shows the place that the crusades were mainly fought over. Do you know where it is and why it is so important to Christians and Muslims?

The picture shows the Dome of the Rock in the Old City of Jerusalem. Jerusalem is the most holy place in the Christian religion. Christians call Jerusalem the 'City of God'. The area where the events of the Bible took place is known as the Holy Land.

But Jerusalem is also a holy city for Muslims. The Dome of the Rock was built where Muslims believe that Muhammad, the founder of their faith, rose up and visited heaven. It is one of the most holy sites for Muslims.

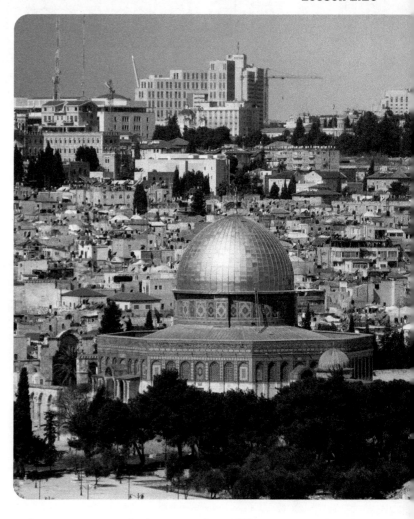

Ever since the time of Christ, Christians have gone on *pilgrimage* to the *Holy Land*. The most important place to visit was Jerusalem, to see where Jesus was crucified and buried. In the 7th century the Holy Land became part of the *Arab empire*. The Arabs were Muslims but, at first, they still allowed Christian pilgrims to visit. Then, in 1071, the area was captured by a different group of Muslims, the Seljuk Turks.

The Turks made it very difficult and dangerous for Christians trying to get to Jerusalem. Tensions rose. The scene was set for the start of the crusades!

Now it's your turn

1 Why is Jerusalem important to Christians and Muslims?
2 Why did tensions grow over Jerusalem after 1071?
3 How does this information help to explain why the crusades started?

Check your progress

⭐ I can talk about why Jerusalem was an important city.

⭐⭐ I can explain why Jerusalem was important for Christians and for Muslims.

⭐⭐⭐ I can give reasons why Muslims and Christians went to war over Jerusalem.

Holy Land: lands around Jerusalem associated with Jesus and Mohammad
Arab empire: the area of the Middle East and north Africa ruled by Arabs

Why did people go on crusade?

Objectives

By the end of this lesson you will be able to:

- explain the reasons why people went on crusade

New rulers in the Holy Land was one reason for the crusades, but historians find there is usually more than one reason for an event. What else made people go on crusade?

Getting you thinking

Look at the picture, which shows two knights about to go off on crusade.

- What evidence is there that they are going on a religious war?
- Can you think of other reasons why they might have decided to go on crusade?

How did the crusades begin?

Alexius I was the ruler of the Byzantine Empire. This was the eastern part of the old Roman Empire and was Christian. He was afraid his country might be invaded by the Turks now they had captured Jerusalem. He asked the Pope for help. In 1095, the Pope called for a holy war against the Muslims to regain Jerusalem for the Christian faith.

Here is what he said:

> Christians arm yourselves for the rescue of Jerusalem under your captain Christ. Wear his cross as your badge. If you are killed your sins will be pardoned.

Western Europe (Christendom)

Byzantine Empire

Constantinople ●

Muslim empire

Holy Land

Rome ●

Jerusalem ●

The First Crusade began in 1096. The idea of going on crusade appealed to Christians in Europe. Many famous leaders went on crusade. The best known crusaders from England were Richard the Lionheart and Eleanor of Aquitaine. Many knights went on crusade. There was even a Children's Crusade in 1212, when 30,000 children from France and Germany set off for Jerusalem. They never reached the Holy Land and thousands were sold into slavery.

Why did people risk their lives to go on crusades?
- Many crusaders were younger sons who would not inherit family lands. They dreamt of wealth and adventure. Ordinary people in the Middle Ages did not normally travel far.
- The Holy Land was a place of great wealth with lands to capture and Christian kingdoms to set up.
- Rulers and ordinary people went on crusade as a punishment for sins.
- Criminals and thieves went on crusade to escape.
- The Pope hoped that a crusade would stop the fighting in Europe and make the church more powerful.

Now it's your turn

1 Explain why people went on crusade.
2 Imagine you are the Pope in 1095. Write a speech to persuade people to join the crusade.
3 You are the younger son of an English baron. Write a letter to your father explaining the reasons why you are planning to go on crusade.

Check your progress

I can talk about what the crusades were.
I can give some reasons why people went on crusade.
I can talk about some of the different people who went on crusades, and their reasons for going.

What was the Islamic world really like?

Europeans went on crusade expecting to find fierce, anti–Christian warriors. You are going to find out if their view of Muslims was accurate.

Getting you thinking

This is what Pope Urban II said about Muslims in his speech when trying to persuade people to go on crusades.

> They have killed and captured many, and have destroyed the churches and devastated the empire.

What do you think the Muslim world was like?

What do you see going on in this picture? It shows a medical examination taking place in the Muslim world. The doctor is taking the pulse of a patient. Compared to western Europe, the Muslim world was very advanced. To the Muslim world, the crusaders were simple and unintelligent people.

The Islamic world was well organised and well run. There was a *Caliph* ruling in each area, giving strong leadership. One Caliph, Harun al-Rashid had a magnificent palace in Baghdad. People living in the Muslim world benefited from law and order, good roads and bridges and irrigation systems. Towns were kept clean and tidy.

Medicine in the Muslim world was more advanced than in the Christian world. In the Christian world, people were relying on magic charms and praying to God to be cured of disease. The Muslim scientist Avicenna (Ibn Sina) wrote a 14-volume encyclopedia of medicine called The Canon of Medicine. It talks about how diseases were spread and even writes about diabetes. Another Muslim doctor called Rhazes (al-Razi) wrote about treatments for measles and smallpox. Muslims translated the books of famous Greek and Roman doctors so they could learn about medicine. They used alcohol as an anaesthetic when treating patients.

Caliph: a Muslim ruler

Many Caliphs were interested in science. Muslims created equipment which they used to observe the stars and planets. Study the picture on the right. You can see the Muslim astronomers using lots of scientific equipment. Education in the Muslim world was excellent and highly respected. Muslim rulers built colleges and libraries in their cities. The number system we use today comes from the Muslim world.

Now it's your turn

1 What is your first impression of what the Muslim world was like?

2 'The Muslim world was very advanced'. Find evidence from the text to support this view.

There was not much evidence to support the Pope's view about the Muslim world. Do you think he would be a good source for telling us what the Muslim world was really like?

Extension work

Take your research further. Find out some more information about one of the following:

Rhazes

Avicenna

Caliph Harun-al Rashid

Check your progress

I can talk about what the crusaders believed about Muslims.

I can describe some of the ways in which the Muslim world was more advanced than the Christian world.

I can describe what medieval Muslims understood about science.

The crusades: a clash of cultures

Objectives

By the end of this lesson you will be able to:

- explain what people from different cultures thought of each other

Getting you thinking

Why do you think that, at first, Muslims and the crusaders knew little about each other? Crusaders called the Muslims 'Saracens' and knew little about their culture or religious beliefs. Muslims knew little about the western European crusaders. They called them Franks and believed them to be ignorant and savage. At the heart of the crusades there was a clash of *diverse* cultures.

This is a picture of a battle during the crusades called the Battle of Hattin (1187).

- Is war always caused by a clash of cultures?

These people study no science and are more like animals than human beings. They lack intelligence and they are ignorant and stupid.

Source 1 *Sa'id al-Andalusi, a Muslim scientist who lived in the 11th Century*

The cruelty of these wicked men goes so far that, thinking the pilgrims have eaten gold or silver, they rip open their stomachs with a blade to reveal if there is gold or silver.

Source 2 *Guibert of Nogent writing about cruelty of Muslims towards Christian pilgrims*

Diverse: different

The two cultures were different. The Muslim world followed the Muslim religion and the teachings of Muhammad. The crusaders were Christians and followed the teachings of Jesus. The Muslim world was much more advanced than the Christian world. As the crusaders and Muslims mixed more with each other during the crusades they got on better.

Source 4 *A Christian and a Muslim playing lutes*

We who were Europeans, have become Easterners. A man who was from Italy or France has become Galilean or Palestinian. The man who once lived in Chartres now finds he is a citizen of Acre. We have already forgotten the places of our birth. Some have married women from the Muslim world. Some have married women who have been baptised. He who was once a stranger here is now a native.

Source 3 *Fulcher of Chartres, who witnessed the First Crusade in 1096*

Now it's your turn

1 Make a list of all the differences between the cultures of the Muslim world and the Christian world.
2 How is the attitude of Source 3 different from that of Source 1 and Source 2?
3 Write a letter home from a crusader to his family telling them you intend to settle in the Holy Land. Show how your attitudes towards the Muslims have changed.

Check your progress

I can talk about some differences between Muslims and Christians.
I can give an example of what Muslims said about Christians, and what Christians said about Muslims.
I can talk about how relations between Muslims and Christians changed.

Was Salah U Din a heroic warrior?

As you have seen, relations between ordinary crusaders and Muslims improved. So, what about their leaders?

Getting you thinking

[Salah U Din was] celebrated for his sense of honour, his generosity and his distaste for bloodshed.

Source 1 *Historians Terry Jones and Alan Ereira*

Source 2 *A painting of the Muslim leader Salah U Din*

This is a picture of Salah U Din, a Muslim warrior during the crusades. He lived from 1138 to 1193. From the source and the picture, what are your first impressions of Salah U Din?

By the 1170s Salah U Din was leader of the Muslim world. He called for a *jihad* against the crusaders. In 1177, Salah U Din's attempt to recapture Jerusalem from the crusaders failed. However, Salah U Din gathered together a very powerful army. In 1187, he won a great victory at the Battle of Hattin. He took prisoner the main crusader leaders, King Guy of Jerusalem and Reynald of Châtillon. He executed Reynald with his own sword but allowed Guy to live.

The victory at Hattin allowed Salah U Din to lay siege to Jerusalem and recapture the Holy City. He let many Christians leave Jerusalem but some crusaders were sold into slavery. Salah U Din ordered Christian crosses to be taken down from Jerusalem's mosques. Salah U Din's armies fought another battle in 1191 at Acre against the forces of the English king, Richard the Lionheart. Salah U Din was defeated. Richard and Salah U Din made a *truce*. They agreed the Muslims would control Jerusalem but Christian pilgrims would be allowed to visit Jerusalem. Although Salah U Din was a ruthless soldier he was well known for his mercy and kindness. In 1191 a Frankish woman's baby was stolen and sold. Salah U Din used his own money to buy the child and return it to its mother.

Salah U Din is often seen as a hero, particularly in the western world, which respected him as a noble, fearless and courageous warrior. In the years after his death, Salah U Din was largely forgotten by the Muslim world. In 1898 a visit by the German king to Salah U Din's tomb helped to remind people of his achievements. Salah U Din came to symbolise the struggle of the Muslim world against the influence of the west. Today he remains a great hero to many people.

Now it's your turn

1 What were your first impressions of Salah U Din?
2 Read the historians' opinion of Salah U Din in source 1. Find evidence which agrees with their opinion.
3 Now find evidence which disagrees with their opinion.
4 Write your own 'Wikipedia' style entry for Salah U Din. Make sure you give your opinion of Salah U Din.

Check your progress

I can talk about who Salah U Din was.
I can describe some of his actions, and what they tell us about him.
I can describe how Salah U Din's reputation has changed, and suggest reasons.

Truce: an agreement to end fighting

Does Richard deserve to be called 'Richard the Lionheart'?

You have seen that there were different opinions about Salah U Din, but what about his opponent, Richard the Lionheart?

Getting you thinking

Have you heard of the king called Richard the Lionheart? He was King of England from 1189 to 1199 and was involved in the Third Crusade. Below is a statue of Richard the Lionheart made in Victorian times.

Richard has been seen by his *contemporaries*, and by later historians, as a superstar – his nickname, the 'Lionheart', says it all.

Source 1 *Historian Dr. Mike Ibeji*

Contemporaries: people who were alive at the same time as the person being described

- What is your impression of Richard the Lionheart from studying source 1 and the statue?

So, did Richard really deserve to be called 'Lionheart'?

Richard had little interest in England and spoke French but not English. Alongside the Emperor Frederick Barbarossa of Germany and King Philip of France, Richard organised the third and largest crusade. In 1191, the crusaders defeated Salah U Din's forces and took control of Acre. Richard's aim on the crusade was to take control of Jerusalem. He once said he would only look at Jerusalem once he had conquered it, but he accidentally caught sight of the city whilst out riding.

The crusaders twice tried to capture Jerusalem but they failed. Richard eventually made peace with Salah U Din. On his way home, Richard encountered terrible weather and landed in Venice. He was then imprisoned by Duke Leopold of Austria who gave him to the German Emperor, Henry VI. Henry demanded a huge ransom for his release. The English people had to pay the ransom. Richard was released in 1194 and returned to England. However, after only a month he went to Normandy in France and never returned to England. He spent the last five years of his reign trying to seize more lands from the French, having abandoned his plans to capture Jerusalem. He died in April 1199 whilst besieging a castle. It was not a heroic death. He was wounded by an arrow because he had forgotten to put his armour on. An infection in the wound killed him.

Now it's your turn

1 Find evidence to support the interpretation that Richard was a good ruler
2 Find evidence to support the interpretation that Richard was not a good ruler.
3 Who do you think was the better ruler, Richard I or Salah U Din?
4 The Bank of England wants to put an image of Richard on a new £10 note so he can be remembered. Do you think this is a good idea or not? Give reasons for your answer.

Check your progress

I can talk about who Richard the Lionheart was.
I can describe some of his actions, and what they tell us about him.
I can decide whether Richard deserves to be called 'Lionheart', and give reasons.

What were the consequences of the crusades?

Objectives

By the end of this lesson you will be able to:

- explain the consequences of the crusades

In the long term the crusaders did not succeed in their aim of capturing Jerusalem. However, events often have unexpected and unintended consequences. This certainly applies to the crusades.

Getting you thinking

After the September 11 attacks of 2001, US President George W. Bush used the word 'crusade' when referring to the 'War on Terror'. His use of the word 'crusade' was widely criticised in European and Arab countries. Why do you think this was?

This is Caernarfon Castle in Wales. Edward I began building it in 1283. How is Caernarfon Castle linked to the crusades?

Mongols: warriors from central Asia with a fierce reputation

In the years after Richard the Lionheart and Salah U Din there were more crusades but they ended by the 1300s. The Muslim world faced a new threat from the *Mongols* who came from the east. In 1258, the Mongols attacked Baghdad and destroyed the city. Other Muslim cities were attacked and ruthlessly destroyed. The Mongol leader was Genghis Khan who planned to rule the whole world. In 1260, a Muslim army managed to defeat the Mongols. Eventually, the Mongols left the Muslim world and new Muslim states were set up. The most successful of these was set up by a Turkish man called Ottoman. He set up the Ottoman Empire and by 1453 the Ottoman Empire had conquered Constantinople (known as Istanbul today). This empire lasted until 1924.

The crusades had a big impact on the world. Many crusaders decided to settle in the Muslim world. The mixing of the two cultures meant that Europeans learnt much from Muslims.

- Castle-building in Europe changed. Kings copied the Muslims' concentric castles with rings of walls and towers. One example is Caernarfon Castle in Wales. Edward I had fought on crusade and was inspired by the castles in the Middle East.
- Europeans took new words from the Muslim world such as alcohol, muslin cloth, almanac, chemistry, admiral, algebra, lemon, orange and safari. Increased trade brought new products to Europe such as sugar, lemons, melons, spices, gunpowder and carpets. The Europeans began to use the Arabic number system.
- After the crusades, there was a renewed interest in science and learning in Europe. This was called the *Renaissance*.

Now it's your turn

1 What happened to the Muslim world after the crusades?
2 What were the consequences of the crusades for Europe?

Now it's your turn APP

You have been asked to plan a TV programme called 'How did the crusades change Europe?' Think of five different consequences of the crusades. Research the two you think are most important. Now you need to explain why you have chosen these two consequences for your programme.

Check your progress

I can describe some consequences of the crusades.
I can talk about some of the ways the crusades benefited Europe.
I can talk about what happened to the Muslim empire after the crusades ended.

Renaissance: rebirth of learning

Who made the rules in the Middle Ages?
Part 1

You have been studying how the king and the church ruled England in the Middle Ages.

Now you are going to carry out a task that will help you to check your progress. Read the instructions very carefully. They tell you what to do. They tell you how to plan your task. They tell you how your work will be assessed.

A medieval king and his soldiers in battle

Now it's your turn APP

You are going to write a short book for a Year 5 student. The title of the book is: 'I want to be a successful king in the Middle Ages'. In your book you will explain what made a king successful in the Middle Ages in a simple way that a nine-year-old child could understand.

Planning

1 Make a mind map to show key ideas.
   Try to find at least four ways in which a king could show that he was a successful ruler.
   Add examples of kings being successful, using what you have learned about different kings.
   Remember that the examples should show how a strong ruler behaved in the Middle Ages, and how a weak, unsuccessful ruler behaved.
2 Plan how you will make sure that a Year 5 student can understand the points you are making.
3 Plan how you will make sure that a Year 5 student will enjoy reading the book.
   Are you using words that the Year 5 student can understand?
   Have you included pictures to help the Year 5 student understand the ideas?

Check your level

I can include at least one way a king could show he was strong.

I can make up a story about a king.

I can use some historical words.

Level **3**

I can include several ways a king in the Middle Ages could show he was strong.

I can give my story a clear structure.

I can use historical terms in my story.

Level **4**

I can show knowledge of changes in the king's power in the Middle Ages.

I can show that I have selected useful evidence for my story.

I can use historical terms to help make my ideas clear.

Level **5**

Read these pages from students' books.

Use the level descriptions on the previous page to decide what level you would give them.

What advice would you give them on how to improve?

Gianni's opening page:

So you want to be a good king in the Middle Ages? Here's my advice. The first thing you must do is to become king. There are several ways of doing this such as being a blood relative of the previous king or winning the throne in a battle. Duke William of Normandy and Henry Tudor both won the throne in battles at Hastings and Bosworth.

What do you think?

What has Gianni done well?

What could he do better?

A section of the Bayeux Tapestry depicting battle

Simon's second page:

Richard II addresses his army

This is Richard II and the peasants.

Once you are king you have to make everyone obey you. I'd advise you to be very cruel indeed. That way the peasants will be too afraid to rebel. If the peasants rebel it would be really bad. You could get killed and then where would you be? If you are really cruel like William I with the Harrying of the North then you won't have any trouble from the ordinary people. The barons used to be a problem too.

What do you think?

What has Simon done well?

What could Simon do better?

3 Ordinary people in the Middle Ages

Objectives

By the end of this unit you will be able to:

- judge how hard life was for ordinary people
- describe the variety in the lives of ordinary people
- show what changed and what stayed the same in the lives of ordinary people

Questions

1 What can you see in this picture?
2 What does it tell you about the lives of ordinary people in the Middle Ages?

der z formofor in multa firipin ramis q
nu peni

Key terms

Black Death a deadly illness – probably bubonic plague

Freeman a person who is free to move to a different village or town

Guild an organisation to protect the workers in each trade in a town

Peasant a farmer who grows enough food for his family

Revolt a major protest against the government

Villein a peasant who is not free to move away from his lord's land

Do you sometimes say, 'I'm bored'? When people today think about the lives of ordinary people in the past they often think it must have been very hard and boring. After all, there was no electricity. What could people do in the evenings after the sun set? Doing jobs must have been slow, with no machinery. It must have been boring staying in their village and having little money. It must have been annoying when they had to do work for the lord of the manor. Historians have studied the lives of ordinary people and they are not so sure about these judgements. See what you think.

Was life good for ordinary people in the Middle Ages?
Part 1

You have spent a long time studying a small group of people – kings and other rulers. Now you are going to find out about the largest part of the population, the ordinary villagers and townspeople.

Getting you thinking

> Compared with a lot of people's lives today, there were times when the medieval peasant had it pretty good.
>
> Terry Jones

This is the interpretation of an historian called Terry Jones. You are going look at a range of historical sources to see if you agree with this interpretation of everyday lives in the Middle Ages.

You are now going to begin an enquiry into the lives of ordinary people in *medieval* times. There were many different types of ordinary people. A few people in England lived in towns. They specialised in different crafts such as leatherwork and carpentry. But most people lived in villages and were mainly *peasant* farmers.

Ordinary people's lives are more difficult to investigate than the lives of the rich and famous. Ordinary people could not write. Historians have to work out what they did and thought from evidence in sources written by the rich.

- What objects belonging to ordinary people in the Middle Ages might still survive today?

- How can historians use these objects to find evidence about ordinary people's lives?

Medieval: in the Middle Ages
Peasant: a poor medieval farmer

Looking at the sources

All the sources below are from books written in the Middle Ages. The books were handwritten as printing had not been invented. This made books very expensive. Usually a rich person ordered the book. Most books were religious: the Bible or a prayer book. They were decorated with pictures. The pictures sometimes showed ordinary people.

Source 1 *A peasant playing bagpipes, from the Luttrell Psalter*

Source 2 *Harvesting wheat, from the Luttrell Psalter*

The Luttrell Psalter was a book written and illustrated around the year 1330. It contains a part of the Bible: the Book of Psalms. The book was paid for by a man called Sir Geoffrey Luttrell who lived in Lincolnshire. It is useful for showing us scenes of peasants and can tell us about life in the countryside in England during medieval times.

- Do you think it would give us a completely accurate view of what the life of medieval peasants was like?

- What can you see in this picture? What does it tell you about life in the Middle Ages? What does it tell you about ordinary people's ideas and beliefs?

- What does the picture tell us about how medieval people pictured *demons*, and how they thought demons behaved?

Source 3 *Medieval nuns, a saint, and a vision of punishment by demons, from the Luttrell Psalter*

Demon: an evil spirit or devil

Source 4 *Medieval warfare*

- What is happening in this picture? What does it tell you about the lives of ordinary people in the Middle Ages?

- Notice that the men with swords are wearing armour, while the men on the ground appear to have no weapons or protective clothing. What kind of event do you think the picture is describing?

Source 5 *Men being punished for adultery*

This picture shows two men being punished for cheating on their wives. They are being marched through the streets and they are naked. What can you see? What does this tell you about how people were punished? What does this tell you about what was seen as a crime in the Middle Ages?

Adultery: cheating on one's wife or husband

Source 6 *A man collecting leeches*

This medieval person is collecting leeches from a river. Medieval people believed in treating illness by taking blood from people. It was known as bleeding. Leeches are small worm-like animals that suck blood and are perfect for this task. Leeches can still be used today in some operations. What can you see happening? What does this tell you about how medieval people treated illnesses? What does it tell you about their medical knowledge?

Now it's your turn

1 Which of the sources support Terry Jones' interpretation that 'the medieval peasant had it pretty good'.
2 Which of the sources challenge Terry Jones' interpretation that 'the medieval peasant had it pretty good'.
3 What else can you learn about everyday lives from these sources?
4 Now write your own opinion of what you think everyday life was like. Remember to include evidence from the sources to support each point you make.

Check your progress

I can use sources to learn about people's lives in the Middle Ages.

I can talk about some of the difficulties of learning about people's lives.

I can decide whether I agree with Terry Jones, and give reasons.

Were medieval peasants stupid?

You have already looked at some evidence about peasants' lives. Now you are going to ask and answer some more questions about the lives of peasants.

Getting you thinking

- Are people who cannot read and write stupid?
- If a medieval person was transported to the present what would they find difficult?

A man ploughing and other farming activities, from the Luttrell Psalter

Medieval peasants did not go to school and they could not read or write, but they knew what to do to survive. Could you have survived as a medieval peasant? Could you grow your own food? Could you make your own clothes? Could you do these jobs without modern machinery? Think about all the jobs that medieval peasants had to do. Which of them need skills that you do not have?

Peasants would also have to know when to do each job. They could learn a great deal by watching their parents, but they would also need to learn to interpret the weather carefully. There was no weather forecast on TV or radio. They could not check on the internet. They had to notice the clouds. They had to notice the arrival and departure of summer birds, when the trees came into leaf and how plentiful berries were in the autumn. How well would you do at forecasting the weather using these signs?

Now it's your turn

Look at the picture. It shows farming activities in the month of March, and the castle belonging to the peasants' lord.
1 What are the peasants doing to help them grow their cereal crops and beans?
2 How could they use their animals to make clothing?
3 How can you tell that the lord is the most important person in this village?

Discuss with a partner:
4 Could you have survived as a medieval peasant?
5 What might happen that would make it very difficult for peasants to grow crops?
6 What problems might peasants have with their animals?

Now it's your turn

1 Write a list of all the jobs a medieval peasant would need to do during the year to make sure his crops and animals survived.
2 You have more knowledge about some things than a medieval peasant had. Which piece of your extra knowledge do you think would be most helpful for a medieval peasant?
3 Explain how well you think you could survive as a medieval peasant.

Check your progress

I can give an example of something I know that would be useful for a medieval peasant to know.
I can give an example of something a peasant could teach me.
I can use the picture to learn about how medieval farmers worked.

What were medieval peasants' houses like?

Objectives

By the end of this lesson you will be able to:

describe the practical building skills medieval people had

Peasants spent their time farming, but where did they live? What were their houses like? Did they have toilets?

Getting you thinking

- Have you planned a project in design technology?
- Did you think of initial ideas?
- Did you research your ideas?
- Did you make detailed plans?

Houses in medieval villages were not planned in the same way architects plan houses today. Medieval people did not understand the idea of a scale plan. They simply used their experience and skills with materials available locally. A series of wooden frames was made from split tree trunks. These wooden frames were called *crucks*. The crucks were strengthened with braces holding the crucks together. Then the crucks were heaved into position using ropes and fixed with beams. The gaps in the wooden frame were filled in with wattle and daub. This was a woven wooden panel with a mixture of mud, animal dung and straw to fill the gaps. The house was thatched with straw, reeds or even heather.

Now it's your turn

Look carefully at the drawing of a medieval village house, then discuss the questions below with a partner.

1 What skills did the builders need?

Think about: choosing and cutting down trees for the frame; sawing the wood; shaping the beams with an *adze*; making joints in the wooden frame; raising the frame; making a waterproof wall to fit in the wooden frame; oiling cloth and making shutters to cover the windows; making a door frame and door; making a thatched roof; putting a hole in the top of the roof for the smoke from the fire to escape.

2 Where would you put the toilet? ·

There was no running water in the house and no drains. The water came from the well outside. It was very important not to dirty the well water with human waste.

- Where would be a good place to put a toilet?
- Where would be a bad place to put a toilet?

The toilet was called a *midden*. The waste collected in the midden was dug out every few months to fertilise the land.

Cruck: the main frames of a house, set in a row
Adze: a tool for cutting wooden beams into shape

Now it's your turn

Draw a flow diagram for someone making a reconstruction of a medieval peasant's house. Remember to include instructions about how to complete each stage of the building.

Extension work

Use museum sites such as www.wealddown.co.uk to find out more about how houses were built and how houses changed during the Middle Ages.

Check your progress

★   I can describe some of the skills a medieval house builder needed.
★★   I can describe the sequence of steps needed to build a medieval house.
★★★ I can put the sequence of steps in building a house in the right order.

Midden: a heap of human and animal dung

Could medieval peasants keep out of trouble?

Medieval villagers had plenty of work to do just to survive, but they also had to work for the lord.

Getting you thinking

Do you have to help out at home to earn your pocket money? Medieval peasants had to do work for their lord to earn the right to grow their own food! Work for the lord was supervised by the *reeve*.

Below is a list of work *villeins* had to do, and taxes they had to pay to the lord and the priest. Villeins had to:

- carry out two or three days' work on the lord's land each week
- work extra days for the lord at busy times of year, ploughing and harvesting
- harvest the lord's crops before their own
- pay the miller at the lord's mill one sixteenth of the grain to have it ground into flour
- pay the lord for permission for their daughter to marry
- pay the priest a tenth of what was produced on their land

A reeve supervising the corn harvest

Villein: a male peasant who had to do work for the lord in exchange for being allowed to farm land for himself

There were many other rules stopping peasants from taking what was not theirs.

- In the forest they could only collect fallen wood for their fires.
- They were not allowed in the forests for any other reason.
- They were not allowed to graze their animals on the lord's land.

In exchange for doing what they were told and obeying the rules, the peasants were allowed land to grow food for themselves. However, peasants did not always accept changes that made their working conditions worse.

> In 1291 all the villeins of the township of Broughton went away from the lord's harvest, leaving their work from noon till night, giving the wicked and false reason that the loaves they were given at midday were smaller than they used to have and ought to have.
>
> **Source 2** *A medieval account of a peasant protest*

Now it's your turn

Discuss with a partner:
- Why did the lords have strict rules for the peasants?
- Were any of the rules unfair?
- What do you think happened next to the villeins of Broughton? Did they get more food, or did the lord force them to work the next day? Use your understanding of life in the Middle Ages to help you decide.
- Which rules would peasants have been most tempted to break?

Extension work

Make a board game for 2–4 players. The aim of the game is to survive the year as a medieval peasant. You should include chance cards to show what could go wrong or help peasants during the year.

Check your progress

I can list some of the rules for medieval peasants.
I can explain why the peasants usually followed the rules.
I can explain why peasants sometimes refused to work for the lord.

Reeve: a peasant appointed by the lord to supervise work on his land

Were townspeople cleverer than peasants?

Objectives

By the end of this lesson you will be able to:

- compare the skills needed by villagers and townspeople
- understand differences in the lives of ordinary people in the Middle Ages

You have now learned about the lives of ordinary people in villages. As you read about people who lived in towns, compare the lives of townspeople and village people.

An apothecary's shop, where medicine was produced and sold

Charter: a document laying down rules for people to follow
Apothecary: a man who made medicines

Getting you thinking

- Do more people live in towns or in villages in Britain today?
- What differences can you think of between living in towns and in villages today?

During the Middle Ages towns grew in size, but they were much smaller than towns today. People who lived in towns were freemen. They did not have a lord and they did not have to do work service. So that he could gain the support of rich townsmen the king granted many towns a *charter*. The charter gave the town the right to hold a market and make its own local rules about trade. Towns with charters were allowed to choose two members of parliament each time parliament met. The richest townspeople were very rich indeed, but were they cleverer than the peasants?

In this book you have already looked at some buildings such as castles and churches which needed skilled craftsmen to make them. What specialised skills were needed to build a castle?

What specialised skills were needed to build a cathedral?

Craftsmen had shops where they sold the goods they made. People in towns differed from people who lived in villages because each man specialised in making one kind of product.

The man who worked in the shop in this picture made and sold medicines. He was an *apothecary*. He belonged to the *guild* of apothecaries. This was an organisation to which all the apothecaries in the town belonged. Each trade or craft in the town had its own guild. The craftsmen trained young men. The trainees were *apprentices*. An apprentice took seven years to learn the skills he needed, then he could apply to join the guild. When he became a guild member he could work for a daily wage or set up his own workshop.

Now it's your turn

1 Look carefully at the picture of the apothecary's shop. What can you see? What do you think were the ingredients of the medicines the apothecary made?
2 Discuss with a partner:
   - Why did it take seven years to learn to be an apothecary?
   - Could a medieval peasant have made medicines like an apothecary?
   - Who do you think was more skilled – a peasant farmer or a craftsman in a town?

Check your progress

I can talk about some differences between peasants and townspeople.

I can compare the skills of peasants and townspeople.

I can suggest reasons why working in a town and in a village were different.

Guild: an organisation to which all the craftsmen in a trade belonged
Apprentice: a trainee craftsman

How healthy were medieval towns?

In the crowded towns, it was a far greater problem than in a village to keep the water supply and the streets clean.

Getting you thinking

- Is it less healthy and safe living in a town or in the countryside today?
- What risks are there?

In the Middle Ages the king's government did not take responsibility for people's health and safety. Think what the problems might be in a medieval town. Where could people find clean water? What would people do with their rubbish? Where would toilet waste go? What would happen if a wooden-framed house caught fire? What other risks and dangers can you suggest? Use this picture of a medieval town to help you.

A medieval town scene

The water from wells and springs easily became too dirty to drink. Most people drank ale because it was less risky than the water sold by water carriers.

Historians can work out from sources that there were problems in medieval towns.

When passing along the Thames, we have seen dung and rubbish and other filth piled up in several places. We have also noticed the terrible smells resulting from this filth. We therefore command you to clean the riverbanks, the streets and lanes of the city of all dung rubbish and other filth without delay.

Source 1 *This is what King Edward III wrote to the mayor of London when he smelled the city as he travelled past on the river Thames*

However, efforts were made to make London and other cities cleaner. People were taken to court for being messy and public toilets were built overhanging the River Thames.

The jury decided that the lane called Ebbegate used to be a public right of way until it was closed up by Thomas at Wytte and William Hockle who built toilets which stuck out from the walls of the houses. From these toilets human filth falls onto the heads of the passers-by.

Source 2 *The city council in York made a rule that no new houses were allowed to have* jetties

Now it's your turn APP

Write a letter from a priest in a town to a village priest. The village priest is planning to visit your town. Tell him about the differences he will notice between his village and the town. Give him advice about how to avoid the problems of life in towns.

Check your progress

⭐ I can describe some of the health problems of living in a medieval town.

⭐⭐ I can talk about some advantages of living in a village, and some of living in a town.

⭐⭐⭐ I can explain why there were more health problems in towns than in villages.

Jetty: The overhanging upper floor of a medieval town house

Could medieval townspeople keep out of trouble?

Objectives

By the end of this lesson you will be able to:

- compare the good points of living in a village and a town
- compare the problems of living in a village and a town
- use evidence to reach a judgement

Was living in towns in medieval England any better than living in a village? Townspeople faced a wide variety of problems in their daily lives.

Getting you thinking

Do you know the saying 'the grass is always greener on the other side'? What does it mean? Medieval villagers often thought that life would be better in a town than in a village, but was it?

A guild master judging two craftsmen's work

Rules in the towns

Do you remember the rules in a village? In the town there was no lord but there were still rules. The rules were made by the town council and the trade guilds. They were different in each town. As you read the rules, think about who would *benefit* from the rules. Would it be the craftsmen who were guild members? Their customers? The richer townspeople? The apprentices? The poor?

Here are some town council rules:

- Apprentices are not allowed to play football.
- No jetties are allowed on houses: they are a fire hazard.
- Butchers must not allow the guts of the animals they kill to pollute the streets.
- Tanners must have their workshops downstream of the town.
- Tradesmen entering the town must pay to sell their goods.
- No-one is allowed on the streets after dark.

Here are some guild rules:

- Guild members must only work the number of hours each day allowed by the guild.
- Everything a guild member makes must have his mark on it.
- Guild officials must check the quality of goods.
- The guild sets prices of goods.
- No craftsman can set up a workshop in the town unless he is a guild member.
- If a master craftsman dies, his widow and children will be looked after by the guild.
- No women are allowed to join the guild.
- No-one may join the guild unless he has trained as an apprentice for seven years.
- An apprentice's father must pay for him to be trained.
- Apprentices must pass a test by producing a 'masterpiece' to join the guild.

Now it's your turn APP

1 Look carefully at all the rules on the left.
2 Draw a table with two columns. In the first write down rules that made life better for the poor in the town than in villages. In the second, write rules that made the town worse than the village for poor people.
3 Continue your letter from a townsman to the village priest. What extra advice can you give him? What advice would you give to freemen in the village who want to move to the town? Should they move, or not?

Check your progress

I can talk about some similarities and some differences between the rules in villages and in towns.
I can describe how the guilds worked, and what they were for.
I can decide whether life was better in towns or villages, and give reasons.

What did people think caused the Black Death?

Doctors today understand about diseases such as the Black Death. They know how it spreads and what causes it. Medieval people did not know what caused disease, but they had plenty of ideas about it. You will be investigating the most serious *epidemic* in the Middle Ages. It was known as the Black Death. In a few years, from 1348, it killed almost one third of the population.

This picture is of a village in Yorkshire in the 1340s. What does it look like now?

Wait and see!

The Yorkshire village of Wharram Percy in the Middle Ages

Epidemic: major outbreak of a disease

Getting you thinking

Imagine if someone told you to pray to God, as that would surely stop you getting an illness. That's what some people said in 1348 when the Black Death arrived in England.

As you read through the sources, find as many ideas as you can about what medieval people thought caused the Black Death. Use what you already know about medieval people to explain why they might find these ideas convincing.

There are two causes of the plague. The general cause was the close position of the three great planets, Saturn, Jupiter and Mars. Such a coming together of planets is always a sign of terrible things to come.

Source 1 *Written by a French doctor called Guy de Chauliac, 1363*

The particular cause of the disease in each person was the state of the body – bad digestion, weakness or blockage.

Source 2 *Also written by Guy de Chauliac*

You are to make sure that all the human excrement and other filth lying in the streets is removed. You are to cause the city to be cleaned from all bad smells so that no more people will die from such smells.

Source 3 *King Edward III writing to the Lord Mayor of London, 1349*

In the year 1348, at Melcombe in the county of Dorset, two ships, one of them from Bristol, arrived. One of the sailors had brought with him from Gascony in France the terrible *pestilence*. Through him the men of Melcombe were the first in England to be infected.

Source 4 *From a chronicle, written at the time of the Black Death*

Now it's your turn

1 Which source suggests that Black Death is catching?
2 Which source suggests that bad air caused Black Death?
3 Which source suggests that *astrology* caused Black Death?
4 Which source suggests medical reasons for the Black Death?

Extension work

Draw a mind map to show medieval ideas about the causes of the Black Death.

For each cause of the Black Death, add an explanation. The explanation should show why medieval people might have believed in the cause.

Check your progress

★ I can talk about some ideas medieval people had about what caused the Black Death.
★★ I can suggest why people believed these ideas.
★★★ I can decide if some beliefs were closer to the truth than others, and give reasons.

Pestilence: deadly outbreak of disease
Astrology: a belief that the movement of the planets and stars affects human lives

What happened when the Black Death arrived?

You have seen what medieval people thought caused the Black Death, but how did they try to avoid it and how did they treat it?

Getting you thinking

When is something frightening?

- Is it when you don't understand what is happening?
- Is it when you can't control what is happening?

Medieval people found the Black Death frightening. They did not know what caused it or how to treat it, but they did have some ideas. Their suggestions about how to avoid and treat the Black Death were based on ideas about causes, as well as what they noticed about the illness.

A medieval vision of the Black Death and its effects

The Black Death affected people of all ages and it spread quickly. Anyone could catch it. Even Princess Joan, the king's daughter died of the illness.

The Black Death had frightening symptoms. Large lumps appeared under the arms and between the legs. They could be as large as an apple. They turned black as the blood within them dried. The victim had a high temperature. Soon blotches appeared under the skin. Within five days the victim would probably die. Some people died very quickly as they caught a more serious version of the illness.

Now it's your turn

1 As you read about how people reacted to the Black Death think about why these methods were used.
   - Soften the swellings with figs and cooked onions mixed with yeast and butter. When they are open treat them like ulcers.
   - Sit next to a blazing fire that draws the air up the chimney.
   - Carry a bag full of sweet-smelling herbs and place it over your nose if you are near someone with the Black Death.
   - Attack foreigners and people who are not Christians. They are probably poisoning the wells where you get your water.
   - Toads should be thoroughly dried in the sun. They should be laid on the boil. The toad will swell and draw out the poison of the Black Death into its own body. When it is full it should be thrown away and a new one applied.
   - Take a whip and beat yourself and others. You will be punishing yourself for your sins so that God will not punish you with the Black Death.

2 Make a pamphlet with advice about how to avoid the Black Death and how to treat it. You must only give advice that medieval people would have given. Explain to the reader why they should take the action you advise.

Check your progress

I can describe some advice medieval people gave for treating the Black Death.
I can talk about who or what was blamed for causing the Black Death.
I can suggest why people might have believed these things in the Middle Ages.

The significance of the Black Death

Objectives

By the end of this lesson you will be able to:

- describe some of the long-term consequences of the Black Death

- make a judgement about the historical significance of the Black Death

The Black Death was terrible at the time, but the consequences did not stop there. The consequences of the Black Death make it historically significant. You will be learning to make a judgement about why this is.

Getting you thinking

Can you remember the ways of judging if an event is historically significant?

Geoffrey Partington's ideas about what makes an event significant are:
- People living at the time thought it was important.
- It changed things very much for people living at the time and made their lives very different.
- It affected many people's lives.
- It affected people's lives for a long time.
- It affects our lives today.

Now study the sources and information about the consequences of the Black Death. Think about its historical significance.

It is difficult to know exactly how many people died. Historians think between one third and one half of all the people in England died. There were fewer workers to feed, but less food was being produced, and other goods became scarce. What effect would this have on:
- the number of workers in villages and towns?
- the wages that lords would have to pay the freemen and craftsmen to work for them?
- the attitude of the villeins who would still have to work unpaid on the lord's land?
- the rent that lords could charge their tenants?
- the prices of food and other goods?

The Black Death returned every ten years or so for the rest of the 14th century. The population kept going down. For another hundred years it hardly increased. The population began to increase again from the 1520s.

This is a photograph of the remains of Wharram Percy, a village in Yorkshire. The villagers all moved away in the late 14th century (see the pictture of how the village once looked, on page 118). Can you think why this might have been?

Attitudes and ideas changed. The churchmen had told people that if they were good they would go to heaven. If they were sinful they would go to hell. They told people that the Black Death was a punishment for being sinful. But churchmen died too. If churchmen died what did this say about them? Were they telling the truth? Was giving money to the church really good for your soul, or did it just make the abbots and bishops rich? We know people began to question what they were told by the churchmen.

Now it's your turn

You are the historian!

Use Geoffrey Partington's ideas for a class discussion on the significance of the Black Death for people in England.

Check your progress

I can describe some consequences of the Black Death.
I can talk about some effects of the Black Death on life in the Middle Ages.
I can decide how significant the Black Death was in history, and give reasons.

Why did the peasants revolt?

Objectives

By the end of this lesson you will be able to:

- explain the reasons why the peasants revolted
- make links between the causes

We might wonder whether medieval peasants liked working for the lords without pay, being forced to stay on the lord's land, or paying taxes. You have seen that they sometimes protested against their conditions, but in 1381 the peasants who lived in south east England went further. They organised a march to London to protest to the king himself.

Getting you thinking

- Do you sometimes get angry? What makes you angry? What do you do?

In 1381 English peasants were angry. Can you think what might make them angry?

Medieval peasants paying taxes

Now it's your turn

Look at the following points. Think about why they made peasants angry? Some points are easier to explain than others! See how many you can explain.

No pay for villeins

Wages rose after the Black Death because there was a shortage of workers. Villeins still worked on the lord's land for no pay. They wanted to be freemen.

Laws about wages

A law passed by parliament in 1351 stated the most a worker could be paid for each job. Employers and workers were put on trial and fined if they broke the law.

The rich were too rich

A priest called John Ball said that God did not create rich and poor. The churchmen had got it wrong, especially when they told the poor to respect their lords and rich churchmen. Why do you think he was imprisoned?

Poll tax

The government needed money to fight a war against France. In 1377, 1379 and 1380 the government collected tax. Everyone, rich and poor, had to pay the same amount. It was known as a head (poll) tax. Tax collection was slow. As soon as the tax collectors finished collecting one tax they started on the next.

Rumours about more tax

When the tax collectors arrived people were confused about which tax they were paying. In 1381 there was a rumour that a fourth tax was to be paid.

The king's advisors

The king was advised about the law by the Chancellor, Simon of Sudbury. Sir Robert Hales, the king's *treasurer*, was responsible for tax. The king's uncle, John of Gaunt, advised him on war.

A young king

The king was 14 years old. He was influenced by his advisors. The peasants thought he did not realise the effects of his decisions on ordinary people. They thought he would want to help them.

Now it's your turn

Draw a series of peasants' heads. Give them speech bubbles. Make each peasant explain one of the reasons he or she is angry.

Extension work

Make a mind map of the reasons the peasants were angry.

Draw lines to show reasons that are linked.

Check your progress

I can talk about why the peasants were angry.

I can explain why poor people felt the poll tax was unfair.

I can show how different events came together to cause the Peasants' Revolt.

What happened in London in 1381?

Objectives

By the end of this lesson you will be able to:

- tell the story of what happened in the Peasants' Revolt
- show how people at the time might have told the story

Chronicles are an important source of evidence for historians studying the Middle Ages. Chroniclers were usually monks, so they were not present at the events they wrote about. They included made-up speeches to show what the people involved thought and why they acted as they did.

Getting you thinking

- Did you know that people often do things when they are in a crowd that they would not do if they were by themselves? Can you give examples of when this might happen? At a football match? At a party?

In 1381 crowds of peasants attacked buildings they would not normally have dared to attack.

Peasants marching behind John Ball

Chronicle: a book recording events that happened year by year

Now it's your turn

As you read about the events of the Peasants' Revolt, look for times when the peasants did things because they were part of a crowd. Try to decide what they were thinking and what their leaders and the king might have said to them.

The Peasants' Revolt

May 1381 Peasants in Essex rioted when tax collectors arrived.

 Peasants in Kent seized a castle and chose Wat Tyler as their leader, and released John Ball from prison.

11 June Kentish peasants marched to Blackheath, five miles south of London.

 Essex peasants marched to Mile End, just north of London. There may have been 50 000 peasants altogether.

12 June King Richard II tried to speak to the rebels but they were too noisy. He returned to London. The rebels attacked palaces and prisons.

13 June The rebels entered London. They were given food and drink by the Londoners. Then they attacked the homes of the king's advisors.

14 June The king met the Essex rebels. He said he would pardon the rebels, grant them their freedom and punish his advisors. Many peasants went home.

15 June The King met Wat Tyler. Tyler demanded that all men should be free and the church's wealth should be handed to the poor. After a scuffle, Tyler was killed by the Mayor of London. The king saved the situation from becoming violent. He agreed to the rebels' demands that they should be free. They went home. They had won!

Now it's your turn

1 Write a chronicle entry for the year 1381.
2 Remember to include speeches showing what the rebel leaders and the king might have said.
3 Try to tell the story from the point of view of the rich and powerful people.
 A chronicler would not take the side of the rebels.

Check your progress

I can talk about what happened in the Peasants' Revolt.
I can write a story about the Peasants' Revolt, from different points of view.
I can write a chronicle account of the Peasants' Revolt.

How much changed after the Peasants' Revolt?

Objectives

By the end of this lesson you will be able to:

- identify changes that took place after the Peasants' Revolt

- find continuity in ordinary people's lives after the Peasants' Revolt

- reach a judgement about whether life was better or worse for peasants by 1500

In London King Richard II made promises to the peasants. However, when they went home he broke his promises. The peasants seemed to have gained nothing, yet by the end of the Middle Ages there were no more villeins and a poll tax was not tried again until the 1980s!

Getting you thinking

Change sometimes happens quickly and sometimes happens slowly. With a partner think about changes that have happened in your lives. Think of examples of changes that have happened quickly and changes that have happened slowly. Did the changes make your life better or worse?

Now it's your turn

Think back to the aims of the Peasants' Revolt. The peasants demanded:

- to be free of the control of the lords
- to have no laws limiting their wages
- to pay lower taxes
- that the king should listen to them

Did the peasants get what they asked from the king?

The king encouraged the peasants to return home by making promises. Later he said the dangerous rebels had forced him to make the promises. This meant that the promise did not count.

But it got worse! The Londoners had to declare their loyalty to the king. They drove any remaining rebels out of the city. Next, the king's soldiers went into Essex and Kent. Rebel leaders were arrested and hanged. Rebellions in other areas of the south and east were ended by the soldiers.

Were the peasants happier by 1500?

Some things did change. The government did not collect another poll tax to pay for war. Although the lords tried to stop wages from rising, the shortage of workers made this impossible.

Although the lords tried to make their villeins work for nothing, unpaid work gradually ended because there was a shortage of peasants. There was plenty of land to go round.

By 1500 all peasants were free. Magna Carta applied to everyone in England.

Life could still be hard. The average temperatures were falling, so farming was more difficult.

Farm work in the later Middle Ages

Now it's your turn

Work with a partner. Imagine you are two peasants living in 1450. You have heard old stories about what has changed for peasants over the last one hundred years since the Black Death. How many changes can you think of? What has stayed the same? Make up a short dialogue that you can act out in front of your class.

Check your progress

⭐ I can talk about what the king did after the Peasants' Revolt.

⭐⭐ I can talk about some things that changed and some things that stayed the same after the Peasants' Revolt.

⭐⭐⭐ I can describe how life was different for peasants by 1500.

What makes the Middle Ages the Middle Ages?
Part 1

People at the time didn't know they were living in the Middle Ages. The period of English history from 1066 to 1500 has only been known as the Middle Ages for about the last 200 years.

Now that you have studied the Middle Ages you have a better idea of what historians mean when they talk about the Middle Ages, but what exactly makes the Middle Ages the Middle Ages?

Assessment task APP

You are going to show how much you understand about the Middle Ages.

To do this you should make a chart or a mind map, covering several different aspects of life. In it you should include evidence and examples to back up your ideas.

Defenders of a castle firing longbows against attackers, who are using a catapult

Here are some suggestions for your chart or mind map.

Aspect of life	Handy hints
Earning a living	What different jobs did people do?
Homes	What were their houses like? Where did people live?
Health and hygiene	How clean were people? What did people understand about illness? What health problems did people have?
The government	Who ruled the country? Were there any changes in who ruled? How did the government control England?
Fighting wars	What weapons were used? What forms of defence were used? How did soldiers attack? Who did the fighting?
Religion / beliefs	What religion did people follow? Were people very religious? What did people believe in?
Technology	How developed was technology for fighting? For farming? For transport? For communication?

- For each one, include evidence and examples of people and events.
- Try to include some examples from local history.
- Try to include some examples from the history of England.
- Try to include some examples from the history of other countries.

Now use your evidence and examples to write an entry for a children's encyclopaedia. It should explain what historians mean by the Middle Ages.

Extension work

Add to your encyclopaedia entry.

EITHER explain what makes the Middle Ages different from today.

OR explain in what ways the Middle Ages were different from another period in history that you have studied.

Check your progress

I can describe some main events and people in the Middle Ages.

I can talk about how different kinds of people lived.

I can talk about who had power and how they used it to keep order in medieval society.

Look at the encyclopaedia entries that Katie and Brogan have written below. Then use the level descriptions to decide how well they have completed the task.

- Which level would you give them for their work?
- What advice would you give them?
- What should they do better to improve their work?

Katie's encyclopaedia entry on beliefs in the Middle Ages:

Religion in the Middle Ages

What did people believe in the Middle Ages? They were all Catholic in England. Everyone went to church and was very religious. They read the Bible all the time. The kings even got crowned by a churchman. If people wanted to get to heaven they did all sorts of things. They didn't want to go to hell because it was horrible there. The monks spent all their time painting pictures in books so it must have been very boring for them. It was even more boring for nuns because they did sewing all the time. I would not have liked being a nun.

Brogan's encyclopaedia entry on war in the Middle Ages:

War in the Middle Ages.

There were many wars in the Middle Ages. It started with the Battle of Hastings in 1066. There were crusades in the time of Richard I. There were two civil wars, between Stephen and Matilda, and between the Yorkists and Lancastrians. The Middle Ages ended with a battle too. At first knights fought wearing chainmail. The Normans used short bows at the Battle of Hastings. Later on longbows were invented. Castles got better too. At first the Normans built motte and bailey castles. At the time of the crusades a new kind of castle was invented. Caernarfon castle in Wales is a good example of what the English knights learned from the crusades.

Check your level

I can show my knowledge of history by describing some of the main events, people and features of the Middle Ages.

I can choose some relevant examples. I can use a few key terms in my writing.

Level 3

I can show my knowledge and understanding of local and national history by describing the main events, people and features of the Middle Ages.

I can show where the Middle Ages fits between other periods of history.

I can organise some of my ideas. I can use dates and key terms in my writing.

Level 4

I can show my knowledge and understanding of local, national and international history by describing the events, people and features of the Middle Ages.

I can show how the Middle Ages fits in between other periods of history.

I can choose suitable evidence to back up my points. I can organise the information to make clear points. I can use a good range of dates and key terms in my writing.

Level 5

4

Power in early modern England

Objectives

By the end of this Unit you will be able to:

- describe changes in the power of monarchs, the church and parliament
- explain when and how these changes happened
- explain the reasons for the changes
- explain who was affected by the changes
- compare the power of rulers in England and India

Do you recognise any of the people in this picture? They include King Henry VIII and his three children. They are the Tudors. They are among the most famous kings and queens in English history. Do you know why? Henry VIII wanted to be known as 'Henry the Great'. Henry's daughter Mary was given the nickname 'Bloody Mary'. After her death people looked back on Elizabeth's reign as a 'golden age'. In this unit you will ask the question: 'Do the Tudors deserve their reputations?' You will find out how important changes were made in who had power under the Tudors and the next two royal families, the Stuarts and the Hanoverians.

Tudor the family name of the English royal family from 1485 to 1603

Stuart the family name of the British royal family from 1603 to 1714

Hanoverian the name of the British royal family from 1714 to 1837

Break with Rome when the church in England stopped being part of the Catholic Church

The English Civil War a war in the 1640s between parliament and the supporters of King Charles I

Questions

1 Can you find Henry VIII?

2 Can you find his three children, Edward, Mary and Elizabeth?

3 Why do you think one of his daughters is larger and nearer to the front of the picture?

4 Find out why this is not a picture that could have been painted from real life.

How did power change in early modern England?

Objectives

By the end of this lesson you will be able to:

- make a judgement and give your reasons
- give examples of similarity and difference

So far you have found out about the Middle Ages. Next you will learn about a period historians call the *early modern age*. It covered the period from about 1500 to 1789. As you find out about it, try to decide what makes it different from the Middle Ages.

Create a hypothesis about the changes that you think might have happened between 1500 and 1800. A hypothesis is a prediction of what might happen. This is usually based upon some evidence, either what has happened before, or new ideas about the subject.

Getting you thinking

So far in the story of power there have been four important elements: The king, the church, parliament, and the people.

Think about all of the events you have looked at. Make a pie chart to show how much power these four elements had in the Middle Ages.

Who would get the biggest slice of the pie? Can you explain why your pie chart is divided in the way it is?

The period from 1000 *CE* to 1500 CE saw many changes in the way England and Wales were ruled; changes in the power of the king, the power of the church and the power of parliament. The next 300 years were to see more events that affected power and the way rules were made in England and Wales. In this unit we will begin to examine some of the most significant events.

A portrait of Henry VIII painted in 1537

Early modern: the period of history from about 1500 to 1800

A portrait of King George III, painted in 1799

Now it's your turn

1 In which ways are the portraits similar?
2 In which ways are they different?
3 What message do you think the artist is trying to give about Henry VIII?
4 What message is the artist trying to give about George III?

Have a look back at your pie chart showing how much power the king, the church, parliament and the people had up to 1500.

Think about the similarities and differences in the two portraits.

Do you think that the amount of power that kings had was likely to have changed or stayed the same in the years between the two portraits. Remember that more than 250 years separate them.

Write your hypothesis:

> *I think that the way England and Wales were ruled is likely to have stayed the same/changed after 1500. I think this because...*

At the end of this unit we will come back to your hypothesis and check to see how good your prediction was!

Check your progress

★ I can describe some differences between the pictures.
★★ I can make a pie chart of how power was divided.
★★★ I can write a hypothesis, based on the evidence of what I've read so far.

Which events were significant in early modern England?

Objectives

By the end of this lesson you will be able to:

- give examples of events that are significant
- explain different kinds of historical significance

This unit is about significant events in the story of power, but how do you decide what makes an event significant in history? You are going to look at some events from 1500 to 1800 and decide what made them significant.

Getting you thinking.

There are several ideas that an historian called Geoffrey Partington used when he was deciding about the significance of events (see page 22). Here are some:

- The people living at the time thought it was very important.
- It changed things very much for people living at the time and made their lives different.
- It affected a lot of people's lives.
- It affected people's lives for a long time.
- It affects our lives today.

Think back through some of the events you have already looked at in units 1 and 2. Which ideas about significance apply to the Black Death? Just one? More than one? Where would you put the Battle of Hastings? What about the Peasants' Revolt? Which ideas are relevant to the crusades?

Below are some events from 1500 to 1800 that are significant. Think about why they are significant.

Event 1

In 1532 Henry VIII split England and Wales from the Catholic Church and changed the religion of England and Wales. This meant, over time, that everyone in the country had to change their religious beliefs or risk death or imprisonment.

Event 2

In 1588 the Spanish Armada was defeated by the English navy, stopping the invasion of England and Wales by King Philip of Spain. This event was celebrated across the country as a great victory, with a service of thanks at St. Paul's Cathedral in London.

Event 3

From 1642 to 1646 there was a civil war (a war between different groups in the same country) in England. It led to the deaths of about 100,000 people. It changed the way England was ruled completely for over ten years.

Event 4

In 1707 England and Wales formed an Act of Union with Scotland and became the United Kingdom of Great Britain, ruled by the same monarch, and with a common parliament.

An early version of the flag representing the United Kingdom of Great Britain

Now it's your turn

1 Think about each event and write down what you think makes it significant.
2 Events can be significant in more than one way. List all the ways in which each event is significant, and give reasons.

Check your progress

★ I can say what makes an event significant.
★★ I can talk about the significance of some historical events.
★★★ I can describe how events can be significant in different ways.

Why was marriage important to kings?

The marriage of Princess Elizabeth and Philip Mountbatten in 1947. Princess Elizabeth became Queen Elizabeth II in 1952

In this unit you are going to look at the changes that Henry VIII made to the power of the king and the church, and what caused him to make these changes (these are called the *causes* of an event). The ways these changes affected the way kings and queens ruled afterwards are called its *consequences*.

In this section we will answer the question: Why was marriage so important to kings in this period?

Getting you thinking.

Work with a partner. Can you think of at least five reasons why a person might want to get married? Why do you think our current queen married?

Cause: the reason why an event happened
Consequence: something that happens as a result of something else

There are five main reasons why kings married in early modern England:

1 Power in England and Wales: If a king married the daughter of a powerful baron this could make him more secure on the throne.
2 Power in Europe: If a king married a foreign princess he could be friends with her country, making England more powerful.
3 Money: Kings could gain land and money by marrying the daughter of a wealthy family.
4 Children: Kings needed a male child to rule the country after their death. This made sure their family kept power.
5 To make their claim to the throne stronger: Sometimes it was not clear who should be the next king of England and Wales. Marriage with the relative of a former king could strengthen the claim to the throne.

How many of these are the same as the reasons you chose?

Now it's your turn

Look at the case studies of royal marriages below and answer the questions.

Henry IV and Joan of Navarre
Henry had been married before and had four sons. Henry had become king in 1399 after seizing the throne by force and spent the first years of his reign fighting with challengers in England. Joan was the sister of the King of Navarre.

1 Why did Henry IV marry?

Henry VII and Elizabeth of York
From 1455 to 1485 two families had fought for the throne of England: the House of Lancaster and the House of York. In 1485 Henry, a Lancastrian, defeated King Richard III, a Yorkist, and became king. He married Elizabeth, the daughter of the Yorkist Edward IV.

2 Why did Henry VII marry?

Henry VIII and Catherine of Aragon
Henry was the younger son of Henry VII. His brother Arthur was the heir to the throne. In 1501 Arthur married Catherine of Aragon, a Spanish princess. Spain was a powerful European country. Catherine's mother was descended from Edward III of England. After Arthur died in 1502, Henry and Catherine married.

3 Why did Henry VIII marry?

Check your progress

I can talk about different reasons why kings married.
I can talk about the reasons why Henry VIII married Catherine of Aragon.
I can decide which reason was most important, and explain why.

Henry and Catherine

Objectives

By the end of this lesson you will be able to:

- identify significant events in the marriage of Henry VIII and Catherine
- organise these events on a graph
- make a judgement about how successful Henry and Catherine's marriage was

You have just thought about why Henry VIII married Catherine of Aragon. Next you are going to find out what their life together was like.

Getting you thinking

Look at this painting called 'The Field of the Cloth of Gold'.

Can you find:
- Henry VIII?
- a golden tent?
- Henry's procession?

What do you think might be happening in this painting?

What clues can you find in the painting that help you to make up your mind?

Regent: someone who rules in the place of the king

Henry and Catherine's life together

Henry and Catherine married on 11 June 1509.

1510   Catherine became pregnant, but the baby was born too early and died.

1511   Catherine had a boy, Prince Henry. He died seven weeks later.

1513   Henry went to France to help the Pope in his war against France. While he was away Catherine was *Regent*. She ruled England and Wales for him. The Scottish king, James IV, invaded England. Catherine helped to defend England, riding north with the army. The English won the Battle of Flodden, killing James IV. Henry defeated the French. The King of France married Henry's sister Mary to help make peace.

1516   Catherine had a daughter, Princess Mary.

1519   Henry had an *illegitimate* son with his mistress.

1520   Catherine's nephew the Holy Roman Emperor Charles V came to England. Catherine helped Henry form a friendship with him.

1520   Henry and Catherine travelled to France and met King Francis I at the Field of the Cloth of Gold.

1521   Henry wrote a pamphlet against new religious ideas that challenged the Pope's power. The Pope gave him the title 'Defender of the Faith'. Henry met Anne Boleyn. She became pregnant with his child in 1533.

Now it's your turn

Plot the events on a graph. On the horizontal axis put the dates. On the vertical axis write the numbers 1 to 10. The better the event was for Henry or Catherine the higher the score you will give it.

Now plot events about Henry in blue and events about Catherine in red.

1   When were things good for both Henry and Catherine?
2   When did Catherine score low on your graph?
3   Do you think Catherine was a good queen?
4   Why might Henry have wanted to end his marriage to Catherine?

Check your progress

I can talk about events in the marriage of Henry and Catherine.

I can suggest reasons why Henry might have been unhappy with his marriage to Catherine.

I can decide how good a queen Catherine was, and give reasons.

Illegitimate: a child whose parents are not married and who cannot inherit a title such as 'king' from the father

What happened when Henry decided to divorce Catherine of Aragon?

Objectives

By the end of this lesson you will be able to:

- identify reasons why Henry broke with Rome
- show links between these reasons

A coin depicting Henry VIII

You are going to find out about the events leading to Henry's divorce from Catherine. To do this he separated the church in England from the Catholic Church. This is called the 'break with Rome'. You are going to explore the causes of this event, asking the question: 'Why did Henry break with Rome and establish a new church?'

Getting you thinking

You have already looked at some events of Henry's reign from 1509 until 1533. Can you think of reasons why Henry might have wanted to end his marriage to Catherine?

The break with Rome: key facts

- In 1517 a German, Martin Luther, wrote an attack on the Catholic Church; he protested that the church was *corrupt* and interested in the rich. His work led to the establishment of a new form of Christianity called Protestantism. This was not led by the Pope.

Corrupt: rotten or dishonest

- Catherine had been married to Henry's brother Arthur. Marrying your brother's widow was forbidden by the Bible, but in 1509 the Pope had given Henry and Catherine permission to ignore this rule.

- By 1527 Henry was in love with Anne Boleyn.

- In 1533 Anne Boleyn was pregnant with Henry's baby.

- By 1533 Catherine of Aragon was too old to have another child.

- Henry and Catherine had only one surviving child, Princess Mary.

- Henry asked the Pope to annul (end) his marriage to Catherine because she had been his brother's wife. The Pope said no.

- The bishops in England supported the Pope and would not help Henry to get his divorce.

- In 1533 Parliament passed laws allowing Henry to divorce Catherine and marry Anne.

- In 1534 Henry was made Supreme Head of the Church in England.

The break with Rome was complete.

Now it's your turn

Draw a mind map to show how each of the following causes of the break with Rome links to at least one other reason.

One link is provided for you, below. Can you find more?
1 Henry and Catherine had only one surviving child, Princess Mary.
2 Catherine had been married to Henry's brother.
3 The bishops in England did not support Henry's wish for a divorce.
4 In 1533 Catherine of Aragon was 48 years old.
5 The Pope refused Henry's request for a divorce.
6 The Catholic Church in England was rich and powerful.
7 In 1533 Anne Boleyn was pregnant.

Causes 3 and 6 link together. The bishops were rich and powerful and they did not feel they had to obey Henry. Therefore they would not help him get a divorce.

Check your progress

I can talk about the causes of the break with Rome.
I can show how different causes linked together.
I can decide which causes were most important, and give reasons.

Henry and the four Thomases

Objectives

By the end of this lesson you will be able to:

- explain how the four Thomases brought about the break with Rome

- weigh up what the story of the Thomases can tell us about who had power in Henry's reign

Henry VIII managed to get his divorce and became leader of the church in England, but he was not able to do this without the help of others. In this section you are going to find out about four men who were significant to this story.

Getting you thinking

Henry could not rule England and Wales without help. Can you think of any areas in which he might have needed help? Here are some clues: money, religion, foreign rulers. What help might Henry have needed in these areas?

The four Thomases

Thomas Wolsey (1475–1530)

Wolsey had some of the most powerful jobs in England and Wales. These included Archbishop of York and Lord Chancellor, the king's most important advisor.

For 20 years Wolsey helped Henry: he arranged the marriage of Henry's sister to the King of France. He planned the Field of the Cloth of Gold celebrations.

Henry turned to Wolsey when he wanted to divorce Catherine. Wolsey failed to persuade the Pope and in 1530 he was arrested for *treason*. He died on his way from York to his trial.

Thomas More (1578–1535)

More was one of Henry's most important advisors; he was his secretary and wrote his speeches. Henry made him the Speaker of the House of Commons. This job allowed him to control what parliament did for the king.

More was made Lord Chancellor in 1530, but he was a strong Catholic and refused to support Henry's divorce. When Henry declared himself to be Head of the Church in England, More resigned from his job and refused to recognise Henry's marriage to Anne. He was tried for treason and executed in 1535.

Treason: a crime against the king or queen

Thomas Cranmer (1489–1556)

Cranmer was Archbishop of Canterbury. He announced that the king's marriage to Catherine was against the laws of God, and married Henry to Anne Boleyn. Cranmer crowned Anne Queen of England and baptised Henry and Anne's baby, Elizabeth.

Cranmer continued to help Henry throughout his reign, writing a prayer book for the new church.

Thomas Cromwell (1485–1540)

Cromwell was an MP and he became Henry's chief advisor in 1532. He helped write the law that made Henry Head of the Church in England and he helped Henry to close the monasteries.

He arranged Henry's fourth marriage to a German princess called Anne of Cleves, but when this failed he was charged with treason and executed.

Now it's your turn

1 How did each of the Thomases help Henry in terms of wealth, religion and foreign powers?
2 Who was more powerful, Henry or the Thomases? How do you know?

Check your progress

I can talk about some of the men who helped Henry bring about the break with Rome.

I can describe something that each of the four Thomases did, and what happened to them.

I can make a judgement about who had power in Henry's reign.

What were the consequences of the break with Rome in Henry's reign?

Objectives

By the end of this lesson you will be able to:

- give examples of how the break with Rome led to changes in England and Wales during Henry's reign
- give examples of ways in which the religion of England and Wales stayed the same during Henry's reign

You have thought about the causes of Henry's break with Rome. Now you are going to think about the consequences of the break with Rome. Some of these happened straight away and some happened long after Henry's death.

Getting you thinking

Who do you think Prince William could ask to marry?

1 Lily Allen, the pop star

2 Princess Charlotte of Monaco, a European princess his own age

3 Kate Middleton, his long-term girlfriend

In fact, Prince William would not be allowed to marry 1 and 2. Princess Charlotte of Monaco and Lily Allen are Catholics, and the King of Great Britain is not allowed to marry a Catholic. This is one of the consequences of Henry's break with Rome that still affects the UK today.

The monasteries

By 1500 the church was very rich, it owned about one quarter of all land in England. In 1535 Henry, as Head of the Church, asked Thomas Cromwell to send out people to find out what was happening in the monasteries. When Henry read the findings he closed 376 monasteries, took their land and treasures and sold them. By 1540 over 800 monasteries had been destroyed. The monks were given pensions, but their servants were turned away penniless.

The Pilgrimage of Grace

In the north of England many Catholics were very angry at Henry's actions. In 1536 Robert Aske formed an army of 30,000 people and marched on York. Henry could not fight them so he promised to pardon the rebels and hold a parliament to listen to them. They went home. Henry immediately arrested the leaders and Aske was executed for treason.

William Tyndale

Protestants believed that ordinary people should be able to read the Bible. Tyndale translated the Bible into English and published it. Henry had him arrested, strangled and burned in 1536.

The Six Articles

In 1539 Henry published the Six Articles of faith. These were identical to Catholic beliefs, except that Henry, not the Pope was leader of the church. The punishment for disobeying the Six Articles was death.

Now it's your turn

1 What evidence can you find that the religion of England changed?
2 What evidence can you find that the religion stayed the same?
3 Was Henry more or less powerful after the break with Rome? Explain your answer.

Check your progress

I can talk about how England changed after the break with Rome.
I can describe some changes to religion in England.
I can suggest how the break with Rome might have changed the power of King Henry VIII.

Consequences for Henry and Anne Boleyn

One of the consequences of the break with Rome was Henry's marriage to Anne Boleyn. This section will examine some of the consequences of this for Anne herself.

Getting you thinking

Read the extract below. With a partner try to work out how Anne felt about Henry VIII at her death.

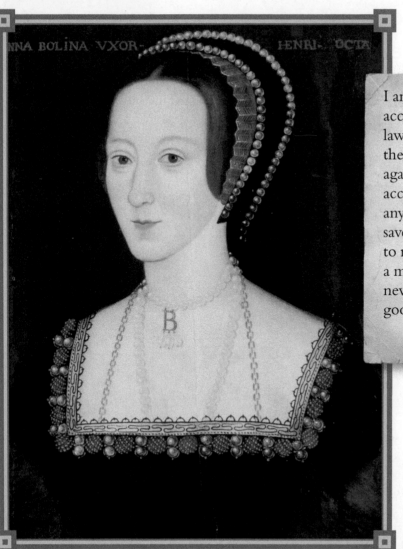

ANNA BOLINA VXOR · HENRI · OCTA

I am come here to die, for according to the law, and by the law, I am judged to die, and therefore I will speak nothing against it. I am come here to accuse no man, nor to speak anything of that, but I pray God save the king and send him long to reign over you, for a gentler nor a more merciful prince was there never: and to me he was ever a good, a gentle and sovereign lord.

Anne Boleyn's last words

Adultery: cheating on one's husband or wife

Anne's family

Anne's parents were both influential figures in the king's court. Her father, Sir Thomas Boleyn, was a diplomat. Her mother, Elizabeth Howard, was the daughter of the Duke of Norfolk, one of the most powerful Tudor lords.

Anne grew up in France but her parents brought her back to England and placed her in Queen Catherine's service. Her father and uncle hoped that she could help the family by becoming Henry's mistress. Her father was soon made an earl and her brother was appointed as an advisor to the king.

Anne's marriage

Henry did marry Anne. She had worked with Thomas Cranmer, her family's former priest, to arrange the divorce from Catherine, and he crowned her in 1533. She gave birth to Elizabeth in September 1533.

Anne was not popular with the people of England, and when she failed to give birth to a son this became worse. Anne probably had three more pregnancies which she miscarried between 1534 and 1536. By this time Catherine of Aragon was dead and Henry had a new mistress, Jane Seymour.

Anne's death

Henry, tired of Anne, began to look for ways of ending the marriage. Thomas Cromwell was told to find evidence against Anne. She was accused of witchcraft, *adultery* and treason. Her uncle ran the trial and sentenced her to death. On 19 May 1536 she became the first English queen to be executed. Henry did not arrange a grave or burial for her.

Now it's your turn

1 Anne is sometimes called the most important *queen consort* in English history. Why do you think this might be?
2 What can Anne's story tell us about the power that women had in Tudor times?

Check your progress

★ I can say who Anne Boleyn was, and how she came to be queen.
★★ I can explain why Anne Boleyn is a significant person in history.
★★★ I can suggest what Anne Boleyn's story says about the power of women at the time of Henry VIII.

Queen consort: wife of a king

Consequences for Edward VI and Mary I

Objectives

By the end of this lesson you will be able to:

- explain the religious changes in England under Edward and Mary
- compare their rule

The consequences of the break with Rome did not end with Henry's death in 1547. His children too had to face the consequences. In this section we will look at Henry's eldest and youngest children, Mary and Edward.

Getting you thinking

Look at the picture. Can you find:
- Henry VIII?
- Edward VI?
- The Pope?

What do you think this painting is about?

Edward VI

Edward was the child of Henry's third marriage. He became king when he was only nine years old and ruled with the help of England's most powerful dukes and Thomas Cranmer, the Archbishop of Canterbury.

In Edward's reign the church became Protestant. In 1549 a prayer book in English was published and churches were made plainer, with no altar or pictures. Priests were allowed to marry and an act of Parliament made Protestantism the only legal religion in England.

It soon became clear that Edward was dying. He was only 15 and had not married or had an heir. The next in line to the throne was his elder sister, Princess Mary, daughter of Catherine of Aragon. She was a Catholic.

In 1553, as Edward lay dying, plans were put into place to stop Mary becoming queen. Lady Jane Grey, Edward's cousin and a Protestant, was named as his heir. For nine days after Edward's death Lady Jane was the uncrowned queen, but Mary gathered supporters and marched to London. The people supported her and parliament declared Mary the rightful queen. The following year Lady Jane was executed.

Mary I

Mary became the first crowned Queen of England in 1553, when she was 37. She was unmarried and soon after her coronation she married Philip of Spain, a powerful Catholic ruler. There were fears in England that her husband would be the real ruler.

Mary immediately started to bring back the Catholic faith to England. Cranmer was burned at the stake and the Protestant laws of Henry and Edward were reversed. Over 200 Protestants were burned by Mary during her reign, earning her the nickname 'Bloody Mary'.

Mary was sickly and was unable to have a child, and Philip spent much time apart from his wife. She died in 1558 leaving England to face a new monarch and more religious change, for the fourth time in 11 years.

Now it's your turn APP

1 What consequences did Edward, Lady Jane and Mary face as a result of Henry's break with Rome? Try to find as many as you can for each of them.
2 What consequences did England face from Henry's death until Mary's death, as a result of the break with Rome?

Check your progress

I can talk about some events during the reign of Edward VI and Mary I.

I can describe the consequences of the break with Rome during the reign of Mary.

I can explain some differences between the Protestant and Catholic religions.

Objectives

By the end of this lesson you will be able to:

- explain some of the problems facing Elizabeth

- show how these problems are related to the break with Rome

After Mary's death only one of Henry's children remained to be queen: Elizabeth, daughter of Anne Boleyn. In 1558 Elizabeth became queen of a country changed by Henry's decision to marry her mother. This section will examine the consequences of the break with Rome in Elizabeth's reign.

Getting you thinking

By 1558 England had been through many religious changes since the break with Rome in 1533. Hundreds of people had been put to death for their beliefs. Mary left the country a Catholic one. Elizabeth had been brought up as a Protestant.

- Should she change the religion again? What might have been the arguments for this? What might have been the arguments against this?

Elizabeth I is one of the most famous figures in British history. She ruled for over 40 years. She did, however, face serious problems during her reign.

Problem 1: religion

Elizabeth was queen as a result of her father's divorce. She made the decision to make England Protestant again. However, Elizabeth knew how much trouble religion had caused her father and her siblings so she wanted to avoid *persecuting* Catholics.

Church services and the Bible were now in English. Elizabeth became Governor of the Church of England. Priests had to swear an oath of loyalty to her. This made the church seem Protestant. However, many Catholic ornaments remained in churches.

Elizabeth declared, 'there is only one Jesus Christ and the rest is a dispute over trifles' and that she 'had no desire to make a window into men's souls'.

What do you think she meant by these phrases?

Problem 2: marriage

The question of marriage and children was very important for Elizabeth, but as a queen the matter was very complicated. Her sister's marriage had proved very unpopular and many believed that the minute a queen married, her husband had real power in the land. Should she: marry an English nobleman? This could make her many enemies. Whom should she choose? Should she marry a foreign prince or king? A Catholic or a Protestant? In the end, Elizabeth avoided marriage altogether, declaring to parliament:

> I have already joined myself in marriage to a husband, namely the kingdom of England.

Problem 3: succession

Without children Elizabeth and England faced the problem of succession. Who would be her heir and the next ruler of England? Her nearest relative was Mary, the Queen of Scotland, who was a Catholic.

Now it's your turn

1. Working with a partner, draw a mind map showing Elizabeth's problems.
2. For each problem, discuss how it can be linked to the break with Rome.
3. Add your ideas to the mind map.

Check your progress

★ I can talk about some problems Elizabeth faced during her reign.

★★ I can suggest why she decided not to get married, and give reasons.

★★★ I can show how Elizabeth's problems were related to the break with Rome.

Persecute: treat someone unfairly and badly

Elizabeth's later years

Objectives

By the end of this lesson you will be able to:

- compare the two problems of Mary, Queen of Scots and the Spanish Armada
- make a judgement about Elizabeth's solutions to the problems

This unit examines two key events in Elizabeth's reign that demonstrate her problems with marriage, religion and succession: the execution of Mary, Queen of Scots, and the Spanish *Armada*.

Mary, Queen of Scots

In 1568 Mary was forced to flee Scotland, leaving behind her baby son James, and seek refuge with Elizabeth. As Elizabeth's *heir* and a Catholic she represented a danger. If Elizabeth died, Mary would become queen and England would become Catholic once again. Elizabeth placed Mary in a series of prisons for the next 19 years but this did not stop plots to place Mary on England's throne. In 1586 Mary was discovered plotting with an English Catholic, and in February 1587 she was executed. Her son, James VI of Scotland, was a Protestant. He became Elizabeth's heir.

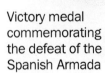

The Armada

This was an attack launched on England by King Philip II of Spain. In 1559 he had offered to marry Elizabeth. He wanted to secure a Catholic future for England. When Elizabeth helped the Protestant Dutch to fight against the Spanish, Philip decided to launch an attack. The death of Mary, Queen of Scots', in 1587 gave more urgency to his plan.

The Armada was launched in 1588 but failed. There were several important reasons for the failure, including severe storms that sank over half of the Spanish fleet.

Victory medal commemorating the defeat of the Spanish Armada

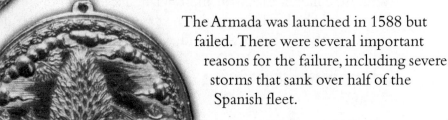

For the English these were signs that God was on their side. The victory medal after the defeat of the Spanish Armada read, 'He blew and they were scattered'. It showed a church on a rock surrounded by waves.

Heir: the person most likely to become king or queen after the monarch dies
Armada: the Spanish word for a fleet of ships

Getting you thinking

As soon as everything was ready for the ships to leave all the soldiers were given two months pay of the seven they were owed …

On the captain's ship is Don Alonso di Lieva, the general of the Spanish fleet, and around 700 soldiers and sailors. They have five pieces of large artillery as well as the guns already on the ship. There are between 125 and 130 ships large and small. The biggest ships are about 73 with 8 galleys. The total number of soldiers are between ten and eleven thousand as well as all the sailors, but rumours are there may be many more.

A letter sent to the English telling them about the approaching Armada

What information can you find in this letter that would help the English to prepare for the Armada?

Now it's your turn

1 How did both these events link to religion, marriage and succession?
2 What can these two events tell us about Elizabeth as a ruler?
3 How good a queen do you think Elizabeth was?

Check your progress

I can talk about Mary, Queen of Scots, and about the Spanish Armada.

I can explain how events in Elizabeth's reign link to the big problems she faced as queen.

I can use these events to decide how good a queen Elizabeth was, and give reasons.

Elizabeth I and the wider world

Part of understanding about a period in history involves understanding how people saw the world beyond their own immediate lives. In this lesson you will find out about contact between England and the wider world in the reign of Elizabeth I.

Objectives

By the end of this lesson you will be able to:

- describe the contact Elizabeth's England had with the rest of the world
- give examples of how these relationships benefited England

Getting you thinking

- What is a pirate? Try to write a definition of one.

Sir Francis Drake

In April 1581, Francis Drake was made a knight by Queen Elizabeth aboard his ship, *The Golden Hind*. He had just returned from an epic voyage around the world, via South America, and presented her with a map of his journey. To the English, Drake was a hero. To the Spanish he was a pirate. He had set out on his voyage to find lands with which to trade and to bring back gold. Much of the gold he found was on board Spanish ships. He stole it, bringing Elizabeth back thousands of pounds in gold at the end of his voyage.

Drake's voyage was just one example of the ways in which England under Elizabeth was beginning to think about travel and trade beyond Europe.

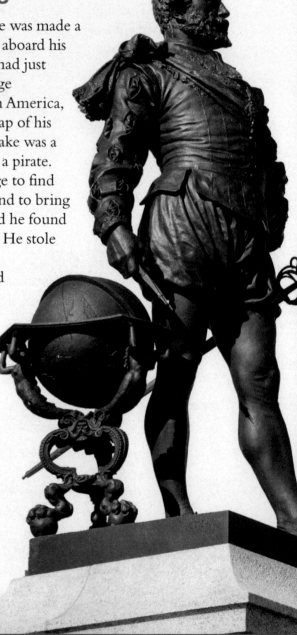

- What does this statue of Drake tell us about how he is remembered by the English? Do you think the Spanish remember him in the same way? Explain why.

Sir Walter Raleigh

Like Drake, Raleigh was a sailor. He helped convince Elizabeth to look to America as a source of wealth.

> If England possesses these places in America, Her Majesty will have good harbours, plenty of excellent trees for masts, good timber to build ships – all things needed for a royal navy, and all for no price.
>
> *Letter from Hakluyt, a friend of Raleigh's, to the Queen*

In 1585 he set off with seven ships to take land for Elizabeth and England. The first English colony in American was founded at Roanoke by Raleigh. After Elizabeth's death many more colonies were established.

The East India Company

On 31 December 1600, Elizabeth granted a royal charter for the establishment of a new company, the East India Company. This was the start of one of the most important trading relationships in British history, that between India and Britain. The company was set up to trade in some of the goods that India had, such as silk, cotton, and spices. The company made huge profits almost immediately, and began to build factories in India to process pepper.

Now it's your turn

Make a list of all the reasons why Elizabeth encouraged so much exploration outside Europe during her reign.

Check your progress

I can describe some of the ways in which Elizabeth's England was in contact with the rest of the world.

I can suggest what the English might have wanted from contact with the wider world, and give reasons.

I can explain what the East India Company was, and suggest why it was so successful.

The Mughal Empire

Objectives

By the end of this lesson you will be able to:

- extract evidence from source material to help you answer questions
- draw conclusions from the evidence you have found

Part of understanding an event in the past involves comparing that event with other events, to examine what is different and what is the same. In this section we will compare Elizabeth's reign with that of another ruler at the same time, Akbar, ruler of the Mughal Empire in India.

Getting you thinking

Source 1

Look carefully at the painting. This is a Mughal Emperor weighing his son in gold. The gold was then handed out among the poor. What can this painting tell you about the Mughals?

Qamargah: a large fenced-off area in which animals were hunted
Cavalry: soldiers on horseback   **Ordnance:** guns of various sizes

The Mughal Empire

The Mughals were Muslims from Asia who conquered land in north India and established an empire there in 1526. This empire grew until it covered nearly the whole of modern India.

Use these sources to build up a fact file about the Mughal rulers. You should look for evidence about:

- how the Mughal emperors spent their time
- how the Mughals fought wars

Three months and six days passed by in hunting: 581 animals were captured with the gun, hunting leopards and using nets. The *qamargah* was held twice; on one occasion in Girjhak, when the ladies were present, 155 animals were killed; and the second time, in Nandina, 110. The details of the animals killed are as follows: mountain sheep, 180; mountain goats, 29; wild asses, 10; Nilgai, 9; antelope, etc., 348.

Source 2 *Extract from the life story of Emperor Jahangir*

He placed the whole of his cannon in front, linked together by chains of iron, in order that no space might be left for the entrance of the enemy's *cavalry*. Immediately to the rear of the cannon, he positioned a line of light camels, on the front of whose bodies small pieces of *ordnance*, somewhat resembling *swivels* in our vessels, were fixed: these the rider could *charge and discharge* whenever he wanted to, without needing to dismount. Behind these camels were positioned most of the *musketeers*.

Source 3 *A report from Francoise Bernier, a 17th-century French doctor who travelled in India*

Now it's your turn

1. Can you see any similarities between the lives of the Mughal rulers and those of the Tudor rulers?
2. Can you find any differences between the lives of the Mughal rulers and those of the Tudors?

Check your progress

I can use sources to find out about historical events.

I can compare sources from different countries to find similarities and differences.

I can use sources to reach conclusions about the lives of the Mughal emperors.

Swivel: *a type of gun*   **Charge and discharge:** *load and fire*
Musketeers: *soldiers with guns*

Elizabeth and Akbar

Objectives

By the end of this lesson you will be able to:

- find similarities between Akbar and Elizabeth
- find differences between Akbar and Elizabeth

Akbar ruled from 1556 until 1605, the same time as Elizabeth was Queen of England. This section will compare them as rulers.

Emperor Akbar receiving visitors within a palace courtyard

Getting you thinking

- What does the extract on the right tell you about Akbar? Do you trust the source? Give reasons.

Early life

Akbar came to the throne at the age of 13. His guardian helped him rule until he was 18, but Akbar was suspicious of those who could threaten his position. He dismissed his guardian and had his foster brother thrown off the palace walls after he was caught plotting.

Akbar faced threats from outside the kingdom and had to defeat the Rajput Empire before he could feel safe. During his reign the Mughal Empire expanded enormously, until it covered nearly half of modern India.

Religion

India, then as now, was a country with many religions. Akbar was a Muslim, but most of his subjects were Hindu. To avoid conflict, when Akbar conquered a Hindu prince's land he allowed the prince to continue ruling on Akbar's behalf. As a Muslim, Akbar was allowed to marry more than one wife, and Akbar married Hindu princesses. His heir was Jahangir, the son of his most important wife, the Hindu princess Jodha Bai.

Unlike previous emperors, Akbar did not want to persecute Hindus: he abolished taxes on non-Muslims and tried to create a new religion which had elements of both Islam and Hinduism. Akbar met with Christian priests in his empire and allowed them to preach and convert people to their faith.

His courage and boldness were such that he could mount raging, rutting elephants, and subdue to obedience murderous elephants. He would place himself on a wall or tree near which an elephant was passing that had killed its *mahout* and broken loose from restraint, and, putting his trust in God's favour, would throw himself on its back and thus, by merely mounting, would bring it under control and tame it. This was repeatedly seen.

A description of Akbar by Jahangir, his son

In the lands he ruled, which on all sides were limited only by the salt sea, there was room for the professors of opposing religions, and for beliefs good and bad, and the road to fierce disagreement was closed. Sunnis and Shias met in one mosque, and Franks and Jews in one church, and observed their own forms of worship.

Jahangir, writing about his father's rule

Now it's your turn

1 What is similar about the way Akbar and Elizabeth made themselves secure on the throne? What is different? Give some examples.
2 What is similar about Akbar and Elizabeth's religious policies? What is different? Give some examples.

Check your progress

I can find one similarity and one difference between Akbar and Elizabeth.
I can find several similarities and differences between Akbar and Elizabeth.
I can talk about how successful Akbar's rule was, and give reasons.

Mahout: a man who looked after a working elephant

What image did the Tudors and the Mughals want to create?

Objectives

By the end of this lesson you will be able to:

- compare and contrast Tudor architecture with that of the Mughals
- explain what impression the Tudors and Mughals were hoping to create for future generations

One of the ways in which rulers try to be remembered in history is by leaving behind paintings and buildings. The Tudors and the Mughals both left important works of art and architecture that give us messages about how they wanted to be remembered and what they thought was important. How an historian understands these messages is called an *interpretation*.

Getting you thinking

Think about Queen Elizabeth II today. We see her image every day, for example on coins and stamps.

- What messages about her is she trying to give in these official portraits?

She has several castles and palaces such as Buckingham Palace, Windsor Castle and Balmoral.

- What do her palaces say about her, and about the people who built them?

The Taj Mahal was built between 1630 and 1653 by Shah Jahan as a tomb for his wife, Mumtaz. It is made from white marble and inlaid with gold and 28 different kinds of precious stones. Mumtaz and Shah Jahan are buried in tombs at the centre of the building.

The Taj Mahal in Agra, India

Interpretation: how something is understood, a way of describing it

Hampton Court was Henry VIII's favourite palace. He spent the equivalent of £18 million in today's money on the palace. It had tennis courts, bowling alleys and a toilet with seating for 28 people at a time! The style of the building was the height of fashion at the time. It is made of red brick with some lighter stone.

Now it's your turn

The Taj Mahal and Hampton Court are both among the most important buildings left behind by the Mughals and the Tudors. They were both built to create an impression. Look at the building materials, the architectural features such as the dome, the windows, the chimneys. Look at the setting of the buildings – the lake and the moat entrance.

- In what ways are the two buildings similar?
- In what ways are the two buildings different?
- What message was Shah Jahan trying to send to future generations when he built the Taj Mahal?
- What message was Henry trying to send by building Hampton Court?
- Do you think Henry and Shah Jahan were successful at creating the impression they wanted to create?

Check your progress

I can say something about the Mughals and the Tudors by looking at photographs of their palaces.

I can suggest why creating an image was important for rulers.

I can explain whether I think they were successful in leaving the message they wanted.

The execution of King Charles I

On 30 January 1649 many people gathered in Whitehall to watch the execution of their king, Charles I. Only just over 100 years after the reign of Henry VIII how was it possible that a king of England could be executed by his own people?

Getting you thinking

In the picture can you find:

- the head of the king?
- a woman fainting?

What do you think is happening in the four small pictures around the main painting?

Objectives

By the end of this lesson you will be able to:

- describe the scene at Charles I's execution
- explain what happened at Charles's execution

A painting showing the execution of Charles I

The execution

It was a bitterly cold day. Charles dressed at six in the morning in two shirts because he did not want to shiver and appear afraid. He met with his priest and then at 2pm the soldiers came for him. He walked to the banqueting hall in Whitehall and onto the scaffold, with soldiers, and the two executioners, waiting on it. The executioners wore masks, wigs and false beards so they could not be identified. Charles's bishop, Bishop Juxon, stayed with him.

Crowds stood below him, held back by soldiers. Charles took a piece of paper from his pocket and began to read. He said his execution was unjust, but that it was God's judgement upon him. He forgave the soldiers who brought him to the scaffold. His last words were:

'I die a Christian according to the profession of the Church of England. I have a good cause and a gracious God. I will say no more.'

Charles put his head on the block: at his signal the executioner raised the axe and severed Charles's head from his body. A man in the crowd recalled that as the axe fell from the crowd there came, 'such a groan as I never heard before and desire I may never hear again'.

Immediately soldiers began to clear the people from the square. The king's body was placed in a lead coffin and under cover of darkness taken to Windsor Castle, where it was buried with no religious service.

Now it's your turn

1 Look again at the picture. It is supposed to have been painted by an eyewitness.
   - Is there anything in the picture that disagrees with the written account?
   - Does this mean the painting was not painted by an eyewitness? Explain your answer.
   - How can we tell that parliament (who had decided upon the execution) was worried that the people might disagree with the execution?
2 Retell the story of the execution from the point of view of one of the people there. You could choose Bishop Juxon, the executioner, a soldier, or someone in the crowd. Think about what you can see, what you can hear, how you feel.

Check your progress

I can talk about what happened at Charles's execution.
I can use the picture to help me describe the execution.
I can find differences between the written account and what is shown in the picture.

How did religion help to cause Charles I's execution?

The public execution of Charles I is a unique event in English history. England had been ruled by kings and queens, good and bad, in an unbroken line for more than 600 years. How is it possible that Charles was put on trial and executed? This section will examine the causes of the end of the monarchy in 1649.

Getting you thinking

Charles I married Henrietta Maria six weeks after becoming king. She was a Catholic. Charles and England were Protestant. Parliament worried about this and refused to allow her to be crowned alongside him when he became king. Why was parliament worried by the queen's religion?

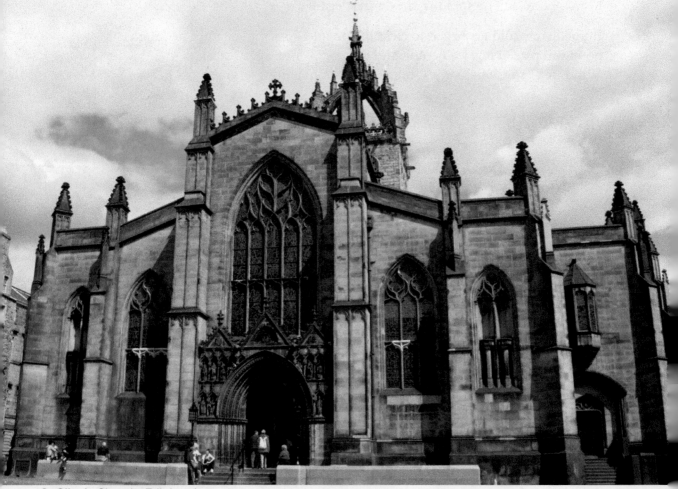

St Giles's Church, Edinburgh

The Puritans

Charles was a very religious man. He believed in the Divine Right of Kings. This meant he thought God has chosen him to be king and he could not be challenged. He changed the coronation oath and promised only to keep the laws and freedoms of England as long as they did not clash with his royal rights.

Since 1530, some Protestants had become more extreme in their beliefs. They were called Puritans. Charles and his Archbishop of Canterbury, William Laud, disagreed with the Puritans. Charles believed that people should be taught about Christianity in many ways, including stained glass windows, music and statues, which the Puritans felt were features of Catholicism. Laud persecuted the Puritans. Many fled to America; others had their ears cut off as punishment.

Jenny Geddes

Charles was also King of Scotland. In 1637 Charles decided to make the Scottish church more like the Church of England. Scotland was much more Puritan than England. When Charles said that the Scots had to use the English prayer book there was conflict. In the church of St Giles in Edinburgh, the dean, dressed in his expensive robes, stood to read out of the new prayer book, to tell the people what God wanted them to believe. For Jenny Geddes, a poor market stall holder, this was too much: a rich man telling her what God wanted! She picked up a stool and threw it at his head shouting 'Ye'll nae say your mass in ma lug. ('You'll never say your *mass* in my ear') Before it had landed the church was in uproar. It became clear that if Charles wanted to tell the Scots how to run their church he would need more than a prayer book. The Scots, known as Covenanters, formed an army. This forced Charles to recall the English parliament which had not met for eleven years, and to raise an army.

Now it's your turn

1. Make a list of the religious problems Charles faced.
2. What can Charles's religious problems tell us about how powerful he was as a king?

Check your progress

I can describe some of Charles's problems to do with religion.

I can describe some of the different beliefs held by people in Charles's reign.

I can talk about what the events of Charles's reign tell us about the king's power, and give reasons.

Mass: Catholic church service

How did money help to cause Charles I's execution?

Kings needed money to rule. James I left his son Charles with serious financial problems. In order to get money Charles had to deal with a group of people he disliked: Members of Parliament (MPs).

Getting you thinking

- Adults often say they haven't enough money. What can they do to get some more? Money was a problem, even for kings, in the 17th century, and Charles I was no exception.

In the 17th century kings got money from their lands and customs duties, but money from taxes was becoming more important. Taxes were raised by parliament so kings had to call parliament and ask them to agree to raise a tax. At the very beginning of his reign Charles and parliament clashed when MPs refused to raise taxes for Charles's expensive raids on France and Spain. In 1628 parliament forced Charles to sign the Petition of Right which promised two things: no-one would be forced to pay a tax which parliament had not agreed and no-one could be imprisoned without a clear reason.

From 1629 to 1640 Charles avoided calling parliament. He appointed a chief minister, the Earl of Strafford, who found ways of raising money without parliament. Strafford went to Ireland and began to make the English colony there more profitable. He 'planted' Protestant landlords, throwing off the Catholic landowners; these new landowners then paid taxes to Charles. Charles raised money from ship tax. It was usually paid only by towns on the coast, but now the whole country paid. Charles seemed to be managing without parliament, but he was building resentment amongst powerful people who felt that he was breaking the Petition of Right. Strafford was hated and nicknamed 'Black Tom Tyrant'.

By 1640 the Scots were rebelling and Charles needed money for an army. He had to call parliament.

Parliament was called in the spring of 1640. The MPs would not give Charles money until their demands were met. Charles dismissed parliament on Strafford's advice. Charles was unable to defeat the Scots and had to sign a peace treaty. He agreed to pay the Scots £850 a day not to fight any more. As a result Charles had to call parliament again to ask for money. This time MPs demanded a price for their co-operation. They wanted Strafford executed for treason. Reluctantly Charles agreed. Strafford was executed in May 1641. One hundred thousand people watched the execution and bonfires were lit in celebration all over London.

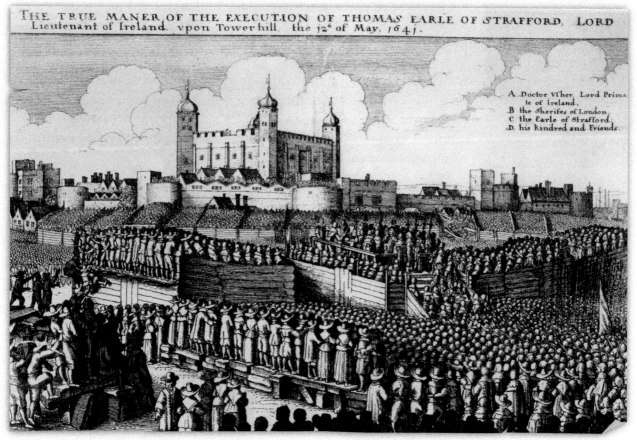

The execution of the Earl of Strafford

Now it's your turn

1 Make a list of the problems Charles had with money.
2 What can Charles's money problems tell us about how powerful he was as a king?

Check your progress

I can say something about Charles's money problems.

I can describe the different ways in which Charles tried to raise money.

I can explain why Charles's actions made people angry.

Which events led to Charles's execution?

The parliament Charles recalled in autumn 1640 was to sit on and off for the next 20 years. It was this parliament that he went on to fight in the English Civil War, and this parliament that ordered his execution.

Getting you thinking

A civil war is when groups within the same country fight each other. England's civil war was in the 17th century. There was a civil war in the United States of America in the 19th century; in the late 20th century a civil war broke out in Europe, among the different groups who lived in a state called Yugoslavia.

- Why is a civil war such a terrible kind of war?

Steps to war

John Pym was the MP who led parliament in making its demands on Charles. In 1641 many laws were passed limiting the king's powers.

The MPs began to go further. Pym proposed abolishing bishops; when Ireland rose up in rebellion against the Protestant landlords, Pym demanded that parliament be given an army to put the rebellion down. For Charles this was too much. Armies were commanded by the Crown not parliament. On 3 January 1642 the king's attorney accused Pym and four others of high treason. The following day Charles himself, with 400 guards, marched into the House of Commons and demanded that the traitor MPs be handed over. They had fled. Both sides began to prepare for war.

By June 1642, parliament had repeated its demands and extended them. Charles said that if he agreed to the conditions he would be nothing but a figurehead.

On 22 August Charles raised his flag in Nottingham and called for all loyal citizens to fight in his defence. The Civil War had started.

The memorial to the battle of Marston Moor near York, at which the king's army was defeated, 2 July 1644

The Civil War

The war split families and killed thousands. One MP was to emerge as a leader during the war, organising Parliament's army and leading them to victory. His name was Oliver Cromwell.

By 1646 the war was over for Charles. He was imprisoned but refused to accept parliament's authority. He still thought himself chosen by God to rule. Not only would he not negotiate, he invited the Scots to take part in a second war against parliament – which he lost! By 1648 parliament's army had lost patience with him. The army forced parliament to put Charles on trial for treason. On 30 January 1649 he was executed.

Now it's your turn

Draw a timeline showing Charles's reign from 1625 to 1649. Mark on it all the events that you think helped to cause his execution.

1 Which events do you think were most important? These can be called 'turning points', events which made his execution much more likely.
2 Mark them on your timeline.
3 Why do you think the English killed their king? Explain your answer.

Check your progress

★ I can talk about how the Civil War started.
★★ I can describe some of the key turning points in the war.
★★★ I can suggest how the events of the Civil War led to Charles's death, and give reasons.

Cromwell the king?

Objectives

By the end of this lesson you will be able to:

- compare the rule of Cromwell and Charles I
- judge how much changed under Cromwell's rule

In January 1649 England, Scotland and Wales were without a king. Charles was dead; his heir, Prince Charles, had fled to France. The man with most power was now Oliver Cromwell, the commander of the army. This section will examine change and continuity: how different was rule by a *parliamentarian* from rule by a monarch?

Getting you thinking

Examine the photograph of the coin. It was *minted* in 1658 showing Cromwell.

- How could this coin be useful to help historians answer the question: How different was Cromwell's rule?
- What clues can this coin give about the way he ruled?

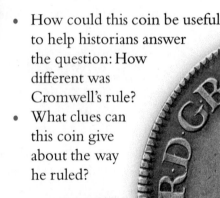

Cromwell and Scotland

Charles had had problems with his rule in Scotland. Was Cromwell able to do any better?

Charles I had been a Scottish king, a Stuart. The Scots hated him because he had interfered in the church, and initially they supported parliament in the English Civil War, but in 1648 they attempted to free Charles by invading England. Most Scots did not support the execution of Charles. They offered the throne of Scotland to his son. He agreed and became King Charles II.

Parliamentarian: a Member of Parliament
Mint: make a coin

This was a dangerous move for Cromwell. In 1650 he invaded Scotland and within a year the Scots were defeated and Charles II was back in continental Europe. The Scots were forced into a union with England and Cromwell's soldiers occupied the country.

- What can this poem tell us about Cromwell's rule of Scotland?

Lament
Scotland is under tribute
To foreigners without justice
Above the right of taxation –
That is part of my sore plight

We are plundered by the English,
Despoiled, slain and murdered;
We must have caused our Father anger –
For we are neglected and poor.

Iain Lom, a Scottish poet, on Scotland under Cromwell

Cromwell, Lord Protector

At first the English government under Cromwell was called the Commonwealth. Parliament soon began to irritate Cromwell and his army. One man, John Lilburne, led a group called the Levellers who believed all men were equal and free. Cromwell had him thrown into prison. On 20 April 1653, Cromwell arrived at parliament with soldiers. He declared 'in the name of God go!' and threw them out. Later that year the army declared him Lord Protector of England. He was to rule with a council and call parliament every three years.

Now it's your turn

1 Draw a table with two columns. Label one 'similarities' and the other 'differences'.
2 Use the information on this page and the pages on Charles's rule, and write down the similarities and differences between Cromwell and Charles.

Check your progress

I can say something about Cromwell's rule.
I can find differences and similarities between Charles I's rule and Cromwell's.
I can describe how much changed under Cromwell's rule, and give reasons.

Cromwell's rule in England and Ireland

Objectives

By the end of this lesson you will be able to:

- compare the rule of Cromwell and Charles I
- judge how much changed under Cromwell's rule

Cromwell's rule was the only time that Britain was a republic, a country without a king. But how much really changed under Cromwell's rule?

Cromwell and England

Cromwell moved into Hampton Court Palace and his daughter was married in the Chapel Royal. His rule of England was very strict. Theatres were closed, dancing banned and the celebration of Christmas abolished. Catholic symbols in churches were smashed.

However Cromwell was relatively tolerant of other religions. Jewish people had been expelled from England 350 years earlier. Cromwell allowed them back. Local churches were allowed to elect their own clergymen. When asked by parliament to become king, Cromwell refused.

Gradually the army was reduced, but taxes remained high. Charles had spent £600,000 a year on defence in the 1630s but under Cromwell the bill was £2,000,000. Cromwell tried to make the country richer; he passed a Navigation Act which said all goods into Britain should be carried on British ships.

He made peace with Holland, defeated the Spanish, winning Dunkirk from them, and he made Jamaica a British colony.

Cromwell and Ireland

In August 1649 Cromwell landed in Ireland. The town of Drogheda was governed by Sir Arthur Aston, a royalist loyal to Charles II. Cromwell sent him a note.

> Sir, having brought the army of the Parliament of England before this place, to reduce it to obedience, I thought fit to summon you to deliver the town into my hands. If this be refused, you will have no cause to blame me. I expect your answer and remain your servant, O Cromwell.

Aston refused to surrender and Cromwell attacked. Cromwell felt he had given Aston a choice and when he entered the town a massacre began. Priests were murdered; the remaining defenders surrendered. They were disarmed and then killed. A group of soldiers sheltered in a church; Cromwell's men set fire to it and they burned to death. The death toll in the town was over 3,000. Cromwell and his army moved on to Wexford, Waterford and the rest of Ireland. By 1652 most of Ireland was under English rule.

Strafford's *policy* of plantation, replacing Catholic landlords with Protestant ones, continued under Cromwell. Two thirds of Irish land was taken away and given to the English. Catholic worship was forbidden and the priests were to be transported overseas.

A portrait of Oliver Cromwell as Lord Protector

Now it's your turn

Use the information on this page to add to the table of similarities and differences you made in the previous lesson.

Now answer these questions:
1 How different was the rule of Oliver Cromwell from that of Charles I?
2 Why do you think England chose to have a king again after Cromwell's death?

Check your progress

I can talk about some of the things Oliver Cromwell did as ruler.

I can describe some positive and some negative sides of Cromwell's rule.

I can compare and contrast the rule of Cromwell and of Charles I, and decide whose rule was more successful.

How did monarchs' powers change from 1660 to 1688?

Objectives

By the end of this lesson you will be able to:

- find examples of how the power of monarchs changed over time
- identify patterns of change and continuity over time

Charles II returned to England in 1660. Britain has been a monarchy ever since. How has the power of the monarchy changed?

Getting you thinking

Go back to pages 136–137. What was your *hypothesis* about how rule in England would change? Did you think the power of monarchs would stay the same? In this section you will get the chance to test your hypothesis. Find out if you predicted correctly.

Charles II (1660–1685)

Charles re-established the Church of England and reopened theatres and race courses. Puritans who criticised this too much were imprisoned. In 1672 Charles wanted to allow Catholic churches, but in 1673 Parliament forced him to sign a new law which said only Protestants could have government jobs. Parliament said Charles needed an income of £1,200,000 a year, but only allowed him £800,000.

Charles and his wife had no children. His brother James, a Catholic, was his heir.

Rumours began of a Catholic plot to kill Charles. Twenty-one Catholics were sentenced to death and people called for James to be banned from the throne. Charles dismissed parliament and ruled without it from 1681 until his death.

A royal portrait of King Charles II

Hypothesis: a prediction of what might happen

James II (1685–1688)

James II promised parliament that he would keep the Church of England even though he was a Catholic. Parliament gave him a large income for an army because Charles II's illegitimate son tried to become king. He was defeated by James. James then began sacking Protestants from important jobs and giving them to Catholics. In 1687 he announced that all laws against Catholics and other Christians not in the Church of England were cancelled. Seven bishops told their clergy not to read James's announcement out.

James's daughter Mary was his heir. She was married to William of Orange, a Protestant. Then James's second wife had a baby boy. Leading Englishmen wrote to Mary and William of Orange and asked them to invade. They did. James's army deserted him and he fled to France.

King James II,
a Catholic king

Now it's your turn

Who had the bigger problems, Charles II or James II? On two sets of cards write the following headings: religion, succession, parliament, the United Kingdom. Give each monarch marks out of 10 to show how well they did under each heading.
- Problems with religion
- Problems with the *succession*
- Problems with money
- Problems with people

Now decide which king was more successful in dealing with his problems, and give reasons.

Check your progress

I can talk about some of the problems facing Charles II and James II.
I can describe the religious problems each monarch faced.
I can decide who was the more successful king, and give reasons.

Succession: the question of who would rule after the king's death

How did monarchs' power change from 1689 to 1727?

In 1688 James II fled England and was replaced by William and Mary. From 1689 to the death of George I in 1727, the role of monarch changed considerably.

William III and Mary II (1689–1702)

Parliament passed a series of new laws setting out the powers of the monarch. No Catholic could become the monarch and no monarch could marry a Catholic. Rulers could not raise taxes without parliament. The Mutiny Act gave parliament power over the army. The Toleration Act allowed churches for most Protestants. In 1692 William and Mary gained Scotland's loyalty.

In 1689 James II landed in Ireland to try and regain the throne. James II was defeated at the Battle of the Boyne and treatment of the Catholics in Ireland got even worse.

Mary died in 1694 without any children, and William died in 1702.

William and Mary: a new kind of monarchy

Anne (1702–1714)

Anne was Mary's sister. She was pregnant 18 times, but none of her children survived to adulthood. Anne was crowned Queen of England, Ireland, Scotland and Wales, and in 1707 the Act of Union was passed giving England and Scotland the same parliament and money. The church and the laws of the two countries remained separate. In parliament two parties developed: the Whigs and the Tories. With no surviving children, Anne was willing to make James II's son her heir, but parliament stopped this.

George I (1714–1727)

When Anne died there were many people who could have claimed the throne. The problem was that the first 50 of these were Catholic. Parliament looked for a Protestant. George I was a German who spoke no English, but he was the grandson of James I, Protestant and the father of two children, a boy and a girl.

King George I with his son and daughter-in-law

James II's son, James Edward, was supported by many people as the rightful king. His supporters, the Jacobites, were mainly Scottish and Irish. He set off to invade twice but never landed.

George was in Germany so much he left his chief minister to run the country. Robert Walpole has become remembered as the first prime minister. He gathered a group of men around him to help him govern; this became known as the Cabinet.

Now it's your turn

1 Make a list of the main changes in the way England, Ireland and Scotland were governed between 1689 and 1702.
2 What things remind you of the way these countries are governed nowadays?

Check your progress

I can talk about some of the problems facing monarchs between 1689 and 1727.

I can describe the way monarchs powers changed over this period.

I can compare the way Britain was ruled in this period with how it is ruled today.

How did monarchs' powers change from 1727 to 1830?

Objectives

By the end of this lesson you will be able to:

- find examples of how the powers of monarchs changed over time
- identify patterns of change and continuity over time

How is your hypothesis about the changing power of monarchs looking now?

George II (1727–1760)

George II spent a lot of time in Germany. Parliament and his prime minister ruled Britain for him. George II was the last British monarch to fight in battle, but it was to protect Hanover in Germany. George also fought a war against Spain in 1739, against the advice of his government.

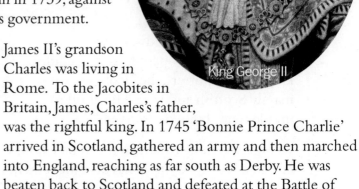

King George II

James II's grandson Charles was living in Rome. To the Jacobites in Britain, James, Charles's father, was the rightful king. In 1745 'Bonnie Prince Charlie' arrived in Scotland, gathered an army and then marched into England, reaching as far south as Derby. He was beaten back to Scotland and defeated at the Battle of Culloden.

George II's new prime minister, William Pitt, helped Britain gain new territory and trade in India, America and Canada. By 1760 George was king of an impressive and expanding empire. George had six children, two boys and four girls.

George III (1760–1820)

George III chose his own ministers. He disliked Pitt and ended all wars Britain was fighting. George was criticised by John Wilkes, an MP, who was arrested and sent to the Tower of London. When he was released he gained compensation. George stayed most of his life in England. He had 15 children. Under George Britain gained a national anthem and the 'Union Jack' as its national flag.

King George III

In 1780 there were week-long riots in London. People were protesting because Catholics had been allowed new rights.

During George III's reign Britain's American colonies won their independence from Britain and the French emperor Napoleon was defeated. George suffered from bouts of madness, and from 1811 parliament ruled with his son.

George IV (1820–1830)

George was not popular. There was an attempt made to *assassinate* him in 1817. As Prince of Wales he spent too much money and secretly married a Catholic widow, Maria Fitzherbert. He was forced to divorce her. He hated his new wife, Queen Caroline. They had no children. They lived separately and she was given an allowance of £50,000. During his reign laws were passed allowing Catholics and Protestants who did not attend the Church of England to vote.

A VOLUPTUARY under the horrors of Digestion.

King George IV

Now it's your turn

1 What happened to the power of monarchs between 1727 and 1830? Did it increase or decrease? Give reasons for your answer.

2 Look back at your hypothesis about the changing power of monarchs (page 137) between 1500 and 1800. How accurate was it? What has surprised you most about what you have learnt?

Check your progress

I can say something about the problems monarchs faced between 1727 and 1830.

I can describe how the power of monarchs changed, and give examples.

I can describe some things that changed and some that remained the same over this period.

Assassinate: murder for political reasons

The significance of events

Objectives

By the end of this lesson you will be able to:

- judge the significance of two events in early modern England
- reach a judgement about which event was more significant

In this unit you have found out about the power of monarchs and the ways this changed over time. You started by deciding what made five events significant. Now that you have learned more about them, you are going to judge the significance of just two of those events. What is the historical significance of the break with Rome and of the English Civil War and execution of Charles I? Why are these two events historically significant? Which is more significant? You will be assessed on your understanding of these questions.

Assessment task

Which of these two events was more historically significant?

- The break with Rome
- The English Civil War and execution of Charles I

Remember to plan your answer carefully.

You could use Geoffrey Partington's ideas about significance to do this:

- Did people living at the time think it was very important?
- Did it change things very much for people living at the time and make their lives different?
- Did it affect a lot of people's lives?
- Did it affect people's lives for a long time?
- Does it affect our lives today?

The ruins of a former monastery, Fountains Abbey, North Yorkshire

Before you write your answer, read the level descriptions in the box below. Use these to help you raise your own level as high as possible.

Check your level

I can describe some aspects of the two events.

I can identify one consequence of each event.

I can make a statement about which event was more important.

I can use some relevant dates and historical words.

Level 3

I can describe the two events in some detail.

I can identify some of the consequences of the two events.

I can use evidence to show the different ways in which each event was significant.

I can include relevant dates and historical terms.

Level 4

I can use the information about the events to explain their historical significance.

I can show some links between each event and its consequences.

I can use evidence to show the different ways in which each event was significant.

I can use relevant dates and historical terms.

Level 5

Below is the last part of one student's answer to this question. How could you help Fabiana to improve her conclusion?

Fabiana's answer:

Therefore the break with Rome was more significant. Everyone was affected at the time and many people have been since. The Civil War has no effect on us today because we still have a monarch. Both were important but the break with Rome was much more important because the country was not ruled by the Pope any more. It increased the king's power a lot. It helped him to divorce his wife and to marry Anne Boleyn. Later on she was executed.

Ordinary people in early modern England

Objectives

By the end of this unit you will be able to:

- describe how those in power looked after the poor
- explain why the poor were a problem for rulers
- describe how the Civil War affected ordinary people
- explain changes in the ideas and attitudes of ordinary people

Many historians think that life became harder for ordinary people in the 16th and 17th centuries. The government took a harsh attitude to the poor, believing that poor people with no jobs could cause trouble and become thieves. When civil war broke out between King Charles I and his parliament in 1642, it seemed as though the whole world had been 'turned upside down'. Parliament no longer showed respect to the king and some ordinary people stopped showing respect to the rulers. This was so shocking that a pamphlet was published about the problem. This picture was on the front cover.

Questions

1 How many things can you spot in the picture that show 'the world turned upside down'?

2 Do you think the things in this picture really happened?

3 Try to explain why an artist might draw these things happening.

What was life like for ordinary people in early modern England?

As in the Middle Ages, the lives of rulers and ordinary people in early modern England were very different. One event however, the Civil War, had a great effect on the lives of both ordinary people and their rulers.

Getting you thinking

- Do you know what the term '*social class*' means?
- What do you think are the main differences between social classes?

What were the different classes in Tudor society?

A Tudor man wrote that, below the monarch, there were four social classes:

- **Gentlemen:** wealthy landowners. 'Gentleman' referred to everyone from barons and earls down to the *gentry* who had the title 'Sir'.
- **Citizens in towns:** included the wealthy merchants and craftsmen.
- **Yeomen:** richer farmers who owned or rented farms. Below them were smaller farmers or 'husbandmen'.
- **The poor and beggars:** included labourers, servants and the unemployed.

Although the lives of ordinary people had changed after the Black Death, in many ways the lives of ordinary people at the start of the Tudor period were not so different from what they had been for centuries.

Over 90% of the population lived in villages and worked in farming. Travel was normally limited to the local market town. The poorest people lived in small houses, with floors of mud covered with rushes and herbs to mask smells. Hunger and disease were constant fears. Most people worked six days a week, with only Sundays, holy days and public holidays for rest and entertainment. Entertainments could be violent by today's standards.

A Tudor writer described how football was played. No wonder that the government passed laws to ban sports like football!

> Football is more a fight than a game. Sometimes their necks are broken, sometimes their backs, sometimes their legs.

Social class: a group with similar jobs and income
Gentry: people just below the nobility (earls, lords etc.) in social rank

Most ordinary people were unable to read. They still depended on the church for their ideas and beliefs.

The local lord would help to control the people in the parish, usually holding the position of magistrate or Justice of the Peace (J.P.). Punishments were very cruel by our standards. Thieves would be branded with an F on their cheek and might have ears and hands cut off. A common punishment was to be put in the stocks or pillory.

The pillory, a punishment for minor crimes

Now it's your turn

In what ways was the life of ordinary people in Tudor times harder than the life of ordinary people today?

Check your progress

I can say something about the different classes in Tudor England.
I can explain what life was like for ordinary people.
I can describe some of the hardships of ordinary life in Tudor England.

What changes were taking place in ordinary people's lives in early modern England?

Objectives

By the end of this lesson you will be able to:

- describe changes affecting the lives of ordinary people in early modern England

Changes in early modern England affected ordinary people, but did this make their lives better or worse?

Getting you thinking

- What do you think have been the biggest changes affecting people's lives since you were born?
- Do you think that change is a good thing?

Early modern rulers were terrified of change. They believed that every creature had been given its place by God in the 'Great Chain of Being'. From the monarch down to the poorest person and the smallest creature, even worms had their place.

Yet, great changes began in the early modern age. A Tudor writer named William Forrest wrote in the 1540s that 'The world is changed from what it has been, not to the better but for the worse.' No wonder that the ruling classes were terrified!

Look at the information below about changes affecting the lives of ordinary people.

Inflation and unemployment

Inflation means an increase in prices. This is fine if you are earning more money. It is not so good if you are unemployed or your wages do not go up.

Prices and unemployment were both rising in Tudor times.

In 1570 it was estimated that 10,000 homeless people were wandering the roads, looking for work and begging.

The Population of England and Wales

1524	2.3 million	6% lived in towns.
1550	2.9 million	
1569	3.2 million	
1600	4.0 million	10% lived in towns

Look at the percentage increase. What effects might this have had?

Religious ideas

For centuries, ordinary people had relied on the church to explain what the Bible meant. Printing meant there were more copies of the Bible. The first English Bible was printed in 1535. The growth of *Protestant* religious ideas encouraged ordinary people to learn to read and to discuss the Bible for themselves.

WILLIAM TINDALL

The newe Testament/dyligently corrected and compared with the Greke by Willyam Tindale: and fynesshed in the yere of oure Lorde God. A. M. D. F. xxxiiij. in the moneth of Nouember.

William Tyndale's Bible, the first translation of the Bible into English, was published in 1535

Political changes

Ordinary people's lives were affected by the Civil War and the execution of the king in the 1640s. Extreme ideas in politics and religion began to spread among ordinary people. Some argued that they should have the vote and be free to worship as they wished.

Now it's your turn

1 Give each of the changes in this lesson a score out of 10 showing how much it would have changed the lives of ordinary people.
2 Explain the scores you have given.

Check your progress

I can describe some of the changes that took place at this time.

I can explain how these changes would have affected the lives of ordinary people.

I can decide which change might have had the biggest effect, and give reasons.

Protestant: a Christian from western Europe who rejected the teaching of the Catholic Church

The Tudor poor: what caused poverty?

Objectives

By the end of this lesson you will be able to:

- describe and explain some of the causes of poverty and begging in Tudor times

One of the biggest changes in the lives of ordinary people in the Tudor period was the greater risk of poverty. The number of poor people increased and after the break with Rome there were no more monasteries to give them help.

Getting you thinking

Did you know that nursery rhymes are often based on real events in history?

Can you work out what this rhyme from Tudor times might be about?

Hark, hark, the dogs do bark,
The beggars are coming to town.
Some in rags and some in jags
And one in a velvet gown.

It tells us about a major social problem that the Tudor authorities had to deal with. There was a great increase in beggars roaming the countryside.

'Hark' means 'Listen'. Why are the dogs barking? 'Jags' were fashionable clothes in which a slit in the cloth revealed a different coloured material underneath. How do you think that one of the beggars might have got a velvet gown?

By 1570 it has been estimated that there were 10,000 homeless people on the roads looking for work and begging.

What caused the rise in begging?

Rulers

- Henry VII had passed a law banning nobles from having private armies. This led to many ex-soldiers looking for work or begging, especially if there was no war on.
- Henry VIII closed down the monasteries in the 1530s. In the Middle Ages, monasteries had provided work and help for many local people.

Changes in farming

Many farmers and landowners changed from crop farming to sheep farming, which needed fewer workers. They also put up hedges and fences around the common land. It meant that poorer people could no longer graze their animals on the common.

The weather

Very wet summers ruined the crops. This only made a bad problem worse! Bad harvests meant a shortage of food and higher prices. Poorer families could not afford to eat.

Population

The population almost doubled in the 1500s; more people were looking for jobs and needed food. Many poor people wandered into the towns in search of work or to beg.

Now it's your turn

Write the beginning of a pamphlet, entitled *The Tudor Poor*.
1 Begin page 1 of your pamphlet with 'Causes'. Explain the reasons why there was an increase in the numbers of poor and beggars.
2 What do you think was the most important cause?

Check your progress

I can talk about the problem of poverty in Tudor England.
I can give reasons why the number of beggars was increasing.
I can suggest what the consequences of increased poverty might have been.

Who were the beggars?

One consequence of the increase in poor people was that beggars became very cunning at finding ways of surviving. You are going to find out about some of these ways.

Getting you thinking

- How do you feel when you see somebody begging?
- Do you ever wonder about what their story is and why they need to beg?

In Tudor times the authorities found it very difficult to decide which beggars genuinely needed help and which did not.

They saw a difference between:

- the deserving poor: the old, the sick and the disabled who were poor through no fault of their own and genuinely needed help.
- the 'sturdy *vagabonds*': those who were healthy but chose not to work.

There were different names for the many types of 'sturdy vagabonds'. Here are some of them:

- ruffler: pretended to be a wounded ex-soldier or sailor
- prigger of palfrey: a horse thief
- angler: a thief who used a stick with a hook on the end to steal clothes off hedges as they dried or objects from open windows
- counterfeit crank: pretended to be sick or crippled to gain pity
- 'Tom of Bedlam': pretended to be mad – sometimes by putting soap and water in his mouth so that it began to foam!

Now it's your turn

In 1566 a London beggar called Nicholas Jennings was caught with a bag of blood that he used to paint fake injuries on his head! In one day he earned two weeks' wages for a workman. What kind of beggar was he?

Vagabond: a person with no home, a wandering beggar

Which kind of beggar do you think that the person in the picture on the right might be?

What can we learn from the picture about Tudor society?

Canting

Beggars even had their own language, called canting. They would speak in canting when they didn't want anybody to understand what they were planning.

Here are some of the canting words they used:

Booze or bowse: a drink or to drink

Cony: a stupid or silly person

Cove: a man or a thief

Glaze: a window

Bit: robbed or cheated somebody or something

Doxy: a woman (beggar)

Darkmans: night-time

Bing-Await: To go away or steal away

Mill: to steal

Ken: a house

- Can you understand the following sentences?
  He bing'd await in a darkmans.
  We have bit the ken.

See if you can make up a canting sentence and try it out on others!

Now it's your turn

It's time to continue your pamphlet, *The Tudor Poor*.

In this section you have to explain the different types of people who turned to begging – the 'deserving poor' and the 'sturdy vagabonds'.

Tell the story of some of the people who turned to begging.

Check your progress

I can talk about the diiferent ways beggars were described.

I can describe some of the different methods of begging used by 'sturdy vagabonds'.

I can suggest why the authorities might have been alarmed by the problem of begging.

How did the Tudors deal with the poor?

There were so many poor people that the government was afraid of a crime wave unless something was done to help. Next you will find out what the government did.

Getting you thinking

John is a Tudor peasant who has been found begging in a town. He says that he has lost his job in his village because of the change to sheep farming. This is the second time that he has been found begging. What do you think the town authorities might do with him?

Punishments for begging included whipping and even death

House of correction: a prison
Parish: the area under the authority of the local church

This is what the Tudors decided to do with the poor:

1 Punish vagabonds and keep the poor in their own *parish*.
The Tudors began to separate out 'sturdy vagabonds' from the 'deserving poor'. Laws said that anybody caught begging outside their own parish without a licence would be punished by being whipped then burned through their right ear with a hot iron. For a second offence they were to be whipped again, burned through the other ear and made a servant for a year. If caught a third time, they could be put to death.

2 Help the deserving poor in a workhouse or in their own homes.
In some towns the council built a *workhouse* for the deserving poor. Here they would be given food and shelter in return for work. If they refused to go into the workhouse, then they would be punished as a vagabond and placed into a *house of correction* 'to learn the *virtues* of hard work'.

To pay for this, the parishes appointed Overseers of the Poor. They collected tax from the people of the parish.

Sometimes, poor people were given raw materials such as wool to work with in their own homes. They were paid for the goods that they produced.

Now it's your turn

Begin a new section in your pamphlet, *The Tudor Poor*. The heading is 'How the poor were treated.'

Copy the statements below and explain whether you agree or disagree with them. Give reasons.

The Tudors:
- were only interested in punishing the poor
- believed that only the parish should solve the problem of its poor
- were too cruel in the way they dealt with the poor

Check your progress

★ I can talk about some of the punishments for people caught begging.

★★ I can explain why some beggars were helped and others punished.

★★★ I can decide whether the Tudors were fair in how they dealt with the problem of begging.

Virtue: good kind of behaviour
Workhouse: place where poor homeless people were sent if they were caught begging

How did care for the poor develop after 1601?

Objectives

By the end of this lesson you will be able to:

- explain how the Elizabethan Poor Law operated after 1601

In 1601 parliament passed a Poor Law using ideas from older laws that had worked well, and from towns which had a large number of poor people. You are going to find out how this law worked.

The Elizabethan Poor Law 1601 pulled together all the previous ideas and made one national system that was used until 1834.

Each parish had to:
- provide raw materials such as wool, hemp and thread for the able-bodied poor to work with
- provide care for those not able to work: the old, blind and lame, often in an *almshouse*
- send the idle poor and vagrants who refused to work to a *house of correction*
- provide *apprenticeships* for poor children
- appoint an Overseer of the Poor to manage the system

The costs for all of this were met from a tax paid by the richer members of the parish.
- How did the law try to make sure the poor worked?
- What measures in the law were the same or different from before?

How did the system develop after 1601?

Rich people often left money in their wills for an almshouse or hospital for the poor and elderly.

The photograph shows an almshouse that was built at Easby, near to Richmond, north Yorkshire. The inscription reads:

'This Hospital was founded and *endowed* by William Smith, Rector of Melsonby, in the 82 year of his age. Anno Domini 1732'

Of course, problems remained for the poor. In 1655 Francis Rawlings, an *almsman* of Price's Hospital, 'being lame and unable to work, and with a wife and four children to support,' complained that his monthly pay had been stopped.

Later laws said that only people born in the parish should receive help from the poor rate. There were exceptions, such as if you worked in the parish for a year.
- Can you suggest why many work contracts lasted only 364 days?

Almshouse: *house provided by the parish for the poor*
Endow: *give money to maintain something* **Almsman:** *man living in an almshouse*

An almshouse in Easby, north Yorkshire

By the 1700s, laws were passed to encourage parishes or groups of parishes (unions) to build a workhouse for the poor to live in. This was thought to be cheaper and more efficient. Even so, most of the able-bodied poor were still found work on the farms and businesses in the area.

The scene was set for the big changes that would come with the Industrial Revolution.

Now it's your turn

Use the information to complete your pamphlet, *The Tudor Poor*. This last section is about 'How the system developed after 1601'.

Check your progress

I can say something about the Elizabethan Poor Law.
I can describe some of the rules that were included in the law.
I can talk about who was not helped under the Poor Law, and suggest why.

Apprenticeship: training in a craft or trade lasting seven years
Almsman: person receiving alms – support from the parish

Caring for the poor

Objectives

By the end of this lesson you will be able to:

- describe how the lives of the poor changed over time

There were always poor people, but the way they were cared for changed over time. You are going to do some 'big picture' thinking to see how things changed over a long period of time.

Getting you thinking

How do you think that each of the following affected the lives of the poor:

- the church?
- harvests?
- laws?
- attitudes?

Now it's your turn   APP

Below are five sources discussing the poor, from the Middle Ages, the Tudor period and the period after 1601.

Your task is to make a living graph about the poor over time.

1 Make cards, labelled Source 1, Source 2, Source 3, Source 4, Source 5.
2 Draw a graph. The title is 'Caring for the Poor'.
3 On the X axis put the centuries: 1400, 1500, 1600, 1700, 1800.
4 On the Y axis put the numbers 1–10 (1 is very unhappy. 10 is very happy).
5 Stick each card on the graph. You will need to decide
   a where it goes on the time axis;
   b where it goes on the happiness axis.

Source 1

The Black Death (1348–49) killed almost one third of the population. This meant more work for survivors. Workers demanded higher wages. Many left their villages to seek a new lord or go into the towns.

Source 2

In Tudor times unemployment increased. Henry VIII closing the monasteries added to the poor's problems. Many roamed around searching for work or stealing.

Source 3

The Tudor authorities passed laws saying vagabonds were to be whipped and a hole burnt in their ear. For a third offence they could be hanged. All *vagrants* were to be whipped until they were bloody and sent back to their own parish.

Source 4

After 1601 each parish had to find work for the able-bodied poor. Those unable to work were cared for, often in almshouses. The rich were taxed to help the poor.

Source 5

A law of 1697 said that all who received help from the parish had to wear a badge on their right shoulder. The first letter was the initial of their parish. The letter P stood for pauper.

The badge for Ampthill parish, in Befordshire

Check your progress

I can talk about some of the laws aimed at dealing with the problems of poverty and begging.

I can describe how the treatment of poor people changed over time.

I can describe times when laws made life better or worse for poor people.

Vagrant: wandering beggar

How did the Civil War affect the lives of ordinary people?

Objectives

By the end of this lesson you will be able to:

- show how the Civil War encouraged ordinary people

You have been finding out about how changes affected the very poorest people, but everybody was affected by the Civil War.

Getting you thinking

So far you have learned how wars affected the rulers of a country. For example, how the English Civil Wars 1642 to 1648 meant that, for a time, the monarchy, the Church of England and the House of Lords were all abolished.

The Levellers' 'Declaration and Standard', a political pamphlet from the Civil War period

- Look carefully at the picture above. What do you think it shows? What do you think the people in the picture are doing, and why might rulers find this behaviour dangerous?

Changes in political ideas

Major political changes didn't just affect the rulers. Ordinary people also began to think about the rights and powers that they had. *Magna Carta* spoke about the rights of all *freemen*. By the 17th century, the peasants were free but only the rich had a say in how the country was run. In the Civil War some people started saying that it was time that ordinary people were involved in making decisions.

The two main sets of ideas that developed during the Civil War came from the Levellers and the Diggers.

- The Levellers believed that most men should be able to vote for Members of Parliament.
- The Diggers believed that everyone had a right to share the land. In 1649 some Diggers seized the land on St George's Common in Surrey and began to dig up the land to plant crops.

Read the extracts below and say whose ideas are being referred to, the Levellers or the Diggers?

`We plough and dig so that the poor may get a living. We have a right to it because of the conquest over the late King.

From a pamphlet published in 1650

We declare that the people shall choose a Parliament once every two years.

From a pamphlet published in 1647

These ideas frightened not just the supporters of the king but also Oliver Cromwell and his army generals. They used the army to crush the Levellers and Diggers. John Lilburne, the leader of the Levellers, spent many years in prison. No wonder that rich people were pleased when the monarchy was restored in 1660, and Charles II became king!

Now it's your turn

1 Why do you think that the ideas of the Levellers and the Diggers were so frightening to rulers at the time?
2 Have we accepted their ideas today?

Check your progress

I can talk about some of the new ideas that came about in the Civil War.
I can explain why these ideas were dangerous to the rulers.
I can suggest why the Civil War helped encourage these new ideas.

Freemen: men who weren't tied to a lord

The impact of the Civil War on women

Men were affected by the Civil War of the 1640s but so were women. You are going to find out how.

Getting you thinking

When we think of war, we often think about men fighting in armies.

- Can you think of ways in which the lives of women might have been affected by the Civil War?

As you read, think about the different effects that war had on women. Some of them were negative: they made women's lives worse. Some were positive: they opened up new opportunities for women. The lives of women at all levels of society were affected.

- Women had to run farms and businesses while men were away.
- Women followed the armies and helped to nurse the soldiers. Some even dressed as men and fought.
- Others called for an end to the fighting.

Most of the evidence we have is about women from rich and important families. Some of the stories are about how they defended their homes and estates. Lady Mary Bankes, her daughters, and their servants, defended Corfe Castle during a three-year siege by parliament's army. They joined other women in dropping stones and hot embers on the attackers.

The Civil War also gave women the chance to become involved in discussing new ideas, in a way that would never have been accepted before. Many women supported new religious groups, such as the *Quakers*, who believed in greater equality.

Others took part in campaigns for political change, such as the Levellers.

It was still difficult for women to be taken seriously, though. In 1649, 23 women called for the release of John Lilburne, the Leveller leader who had been placed in prison. They were told to go home and wash the dishes!

The picture on the right is called 'The Parliament of Women'. It was drawn in 1646 to make fun of women's demands to be involved in politics.

Quakers: a religious group that began just after the Civil War

The Parliament of Women

The words that went with the picture read: 'With the merry laws by them newly enacted. To live in more *ease*, *pomp*, pride and *wantonness*, but, especially, that they might have superiority and domineer over their husbands.'

- How can you tell that the writer is making fun of the idea of a parliament of women?

Now it's your turn

Write an article entitled *Women in the Civil War*. You need to refer to:
- extra responsibilities that women had
- women and fighting
- women and new ideas
- how women were not always taken seriously

What do you think happened to women's lives when the Civil War ended?

Check your progress

I can talk about how the Civil War affected women's lives.

I can describe some of the new things women were involved in during the Civil War.

I can suggest what might have happened to women's lives after the Civil War ended.

Ease: relaxation, comfort   **Pomp:** *magnificence, grandeur*
Wantonness: loose or shameful living

New religious ideas

Objectives

By the end of this lesson you will be able to:

- explain how the Church of England stopped being the only Protestant church in England

In the Civil War period it was harder for the rulers to control what was happening. Printing was cheap and many pamphlets were published with shocking new religious ideas. The consequences were enormous.

Getting you thinking

- How many different churches can you think of in your town or area?
- When do you think it changed from one church to many, and how?

Before the Civil War there had been only one church. By Elizabeth's reign people could be fined for not attending church or even killed if they tried to worship in a different way.

In September 1558 Richard Snell, a weaver from Bedale in Yorkshire, was burnt at the stake because he would not accept the Roman Catholic faith of Queen Mary.

Nowadays, there are many different churches. How did this come about? Big changes took place during the Civil War.

- King Charles I had helped to cause the Civil War because people thought that he wanted to make the church more like the Catholic Church. The strongest opponents were Puritans, extreme Protestants who wanted a simple church.
- When parliament's army defeated and executed the king, they decided to get rid of the Church of England and allow different kinds of Christian worship. As long as it wasn't Catholic, of course! Many different types of religious ideas began to develop. One such group that still exists are the Quakers.

Who were the Quakers?

George Fox started the Quakers, or Society of Friends, in the 1650s. Fox's travels around England made him question the way in which God was worshipped in church services. He came to believe that:

- you did not need strict rules and services to worship God
- Christ was inside all Christians so that everybody was equal
- there was no need for bishops, ministers or a special church building. All men and women could be ministers

The Quakers worried many people at the time, especially the rich and powerful. Can you think why? Can you think why many women were attracted to the Quakers?

George Fox

After 1660 when the Church of England was restored, the authorities tried to crush the Quakers, but it was not possible. Eventually, in 1689, King William III allowed people (except Catholics) to worship in their own way and no longer tried to force everybody to worship in the Church of England. Since then, we have had different churches in England alongside the Church of England.

Now it's your turn

Write a speech, either for or against the Quakers, that might have been written in the 1650s.

Check your progress

I can list some of the churches that exist today.
I can describe some of the views of the Quakers.
I can explain why the Quakers' views might have worried the rich and powerful.

What was the most significant event between 1066 and 1660? Part 1

Objectives

By the end of this lesson you will be able to:

- choose which event is most significant
- explain why you think an event is historically significant

Getting you thinking

- How many different historical events can you think of which took place between 1066 and 1660?

Below is a photograph of the British Museum in London. It is a world famous museum which houses many famous historical artefacts.

Imagine the British Museum is giving you a room to dedicate to an historical event that took place between 1066 and 1660. You need to decide which event was the most significant one to have in your museum room.

Remember to think about how you judge whether an event is significant (see page 20).

Events to choose from

1 Battle of Hastings (1066)
The Normans win the Battle of Hastings and William the Conqueror becomes the King of England. Castles are built across England and the Anglo–Saxon line of kings is broken.

2 Magna Carta (1215)
King John signs the Magna Carta after pressure from his rebels. This important document starts parliament and gives basic rights to the people.

3 The Battle of Hattin (1187)
Salah U Din defeats a crusader army and Jerusalem and the Holy Land are lost by the Christian knights.

4 The Black Death (1348)
This terrible disease kills one third of the population of England. For those who are left behind life gets better as fewer people compete for resources.

5 The Peasants' Revolt (1381)
Wat Tyler leads rebellion of peasants. It is stopped by Richard II but the event helps bring about more freedoms for ordinary people in England.

6 The break with Rome (1536)
Henry VIII breaks the power of the Catholic Church in England and the country becomes Protestant. This leads to the dissolution of monasteries across the country.

7 The Gunpowder Plot (1605)
A plot led by Robert Catesby and carried out by Guy Fawkes tries, unsuccessfully, to blow up the Houses of Parliament and kill King James I.

8 The execution of King Charles I (1649)
After years of civil war, the English execute their king, Charles I, and for the next 11 years the country is ruled without a king.

Assessment activity
Part 1: Historical significance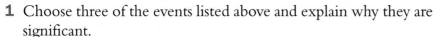

1 Choose three of the events listed above and explain why they are significant.
2 Write a letter to the head of the British Museum suggesting a new exhibition, looking at at one of the events from the list. Explain why you have chosen this event and what kind of objects and pictures they might include in the exhibition.

You will need to do the following in your letter:
- Explain why your event is so significant.
- Explain why it is more significant than the other events.
- Use formal language.

What was the most significant event between 1066 and 1660? Part 2

Objectives

By the end of this lesson you will be able to:

- make a judgement about what level a piece of work is
- suggest how a piece of work can be improved

Hans, Edward and Maria have been asked to do the same exercise. Read their letters, then answer the questions that follow.

Hans

The Gunpowder Plot was the most significant event. Guy Fawkes tried to kill the king. This is the most significant because every year I enjoy Bonfire Night and I always have a great time.

Edward

Dear Sir

We should definitely have a room set up to show how significant the Battle of Hastings was. I think this would be great! It was significant because William, Duke of Normandy killed Harold Godwinson. It was a significant event because England was taken over by the Normans and lots of castles such as the Tower of London were built. England was changed forever.

Maria

> Dear Sir
>
> Thank you for giving me the opportunity to set up a room in the British Museum. I am writing to explain why I have chosen Henry VIII's break with Rome.
>
> One of the ways that historians consider significance is to see if it affects our lives today. Many of the other events such as the Black Death do not affect our lives today. However, if it were not for the break with Rome taking place, then we would not have the Church of England today.

Now it's your turn

1 Using the 'Check your level' box as a guide, decide what level Hans, Edward and Maria have reached in their answers.
2 Look at Hans's answer. What advice could you give him to improve his answer?
3 Look at the letter you have written. Give it a level. What could you do to improve it?

Check your level

I can include some knowledge of the event

I can give a few reasons why the event is significant.

Level 3

I can show detailed knowledge of the event.

I can give my letter a clear structure.

I can give some reasons for why your event is significant.

Level 4

I can show detailed knowledge of the event.

I can give my letter a clear structure and use appropriate language.

I can give detailed reasons why my event is significant.

Level 5

How can I find out more about history?

Getting you thinking

Source 1

What do you think is going on in this picture? It looks like a battle from the English Civil War. It is a picture of a re-enactment society acting out a battle in the 21st century. There are many re-enactment societies, where people can experience different battles and events. Do you think this would be a good way for finding out about the past?

Consider the following sources and decide how useful they are for telling us about the past.

Source 2 *An advert for a Tudor style feast*

Come to our castle for the real experience of a medieval banquet!

Enjoy a traditional medieval meal of roast meats, jacket potatoes and seasonal vegetables (vegetarian option available). Mead and wine are served with the meal. Finish the meal with coffee and mints. Your host for the evening is King Henry VIII. Ladies of the court in costume, along with jesters, will entertain you. Dance the night away at the medieval discotheque. Guests can also wear costume if they choose.

Fountains Abbey was one of the monasteries *dissolved* in the 1530s. Today, Fountains Abbey is owned by the National Trust. The National Trust is an organisation that owns many historic buildings and helps preserve them so people can visit them.

Source 3 *Fountains Abbey in Yorkshire*

Now it's your turn

1 What can each historical source tell us about the past?
2 Which historical source do you think would be most useful for telling us about the past?

Assessment activity
Part 2: Historical enquiry APP

You have already written a letter to the head of the British Museum about the event you have chosen for your room in the museum.

You enquiry task is to choose the objects that you will display, and the sources (words and pictures) that you will include.

As you find sources, use a grid to record:
- what evidence the source contains
- whether the evidence is different from that in other sources
- what the evidence tells you – why it is useful
- any problems with the source

Now make a plan of how the room will be set out, showing where each source and each object you have chosen will displayed.

Extension work

Write information cards to go beside the sources and objects. Each card should give some details about the item and what it shows.

Check your progress

I can choose sources to answer questions about the past.

I can put together information from different sources to answer questions.

I can use my knowledge and understanding to decide which sources are most useful.

Dissolve: used here, this means to close a monastery and take away its possessions

How much did life change between 1066 and 1660?

Objectives

By the end of this lesson you will be able to:

* desribe how much life changed
* give reasons why change took place

The England of 1066 and 1660 are separated by almost 600 years. How many changes took place during this period?

Getting you thinking

The execution of Charles I in 1649 turned 17th century England 'upside down', but by 1660 England had restored the monarchy. Sometimes, things in history stay the same.

Six hundred years before, another king called Harold Godwinson had been forced off the throne. So, how much did life really change between 1066 and 1660?

England in 1066

England was ruled by King William I. He became king after winning the Battle of Hastings. England, Wales, Scotland and Ireland were separate kingdoms. The king was powerful and ran the country with his Norman supporters.

Ordinary people lived in villages and worked in farming. Women were not thought to be as important as men and were expected to obey male relatives. Medical knowledge was simple and *life expectancy* was low – people lived, on average, until their late 30s. People were Catholics and loyal to the Pope. The Normans built great cathedrals and the church was used to control people. England was a diverse place, having been invaded by Anglo-Saxons, Vikings and Normans. King William encouraged Jewish merchants to move to England.

The population of England was more than one million. People knew little about science and the wider world, and did not know continents like America and Australia existed.

Life expectancy: how long people lived, on average

England in 1660

England was ruled by King Charles II. He became king after the monarchy was restored. England and Wales were united, but Scotland and Ireland were separate kingdoms. The king was less powerful and parliament was becoming more powerful.

Most ordinary people worked in farming although some people made money as merchants. Women were not thought to be as important as men and some women had been accused of witchcraft. England was unhealthy and illnesses such as the plague were common. Life expectancy was around 40. Most people were Protestants. People were not allowed to be Catholic. England was a diverse place, with people travelling to trade, and black slaves living in English households. In the 1650s Oliver Cromwell allowed Jewish people to return to England after they had been expelled in 1290 by King Edward I.

King Charles II

The population of England was around five million. People knew more about science and the world. Some people left England to start a new life in the 'New World' American colonies.

Now it's your turn APP

1 Make a list of the differences in England between 1066 and 1660.
2 Make a list of what stayed the same in England between 1066 and 1660.
3 How much do you think life changed for people between 1066 and 1660?

Check your progress

I can give example of changes in England between 1066 and 1660.
I can give examples of things that stayed the same.
I can describe how much life changed for ordinary people, and give examples.

England in 1750

Key terms

Great Britain a country made up of Wales, Scotland and England

Empire a collection of countries ruled over by one national group

Britain in 1750 was very different from England in 1066. England and Scotland were united, as Great Britain, under one monarch. Parliament was much more powerful than in 1066. The king was king of Great Britain. Most people were still Christian, but a range of different forms of Protestant Christianity were allowed. Most people still lived in villages, but towns were growing quickly. Industry was beginning to develop. Britain's links with the wider world were changing. Britain was beginning to gain an overseas empire. In 1750 Britain was poised to become the first industrial nation with the largest empire the world had ever seen. This is what you will go on to study.

Questions

What clues can you find in this picture to support the view that 'England was poised to become the first industrial nation'?

Glossary

Abbot: the monk in charge of a monastery or abbey

Adultery: cheating on one's wife or husband

Adze: a tool for cutting wooden beams into shape

Almshouse: house provided by the parish for the poor

Almsman: person receiving alms – support from the parish

Anachronism: an object which appears in the wrong time period

Apothecary: a man who made medicines

Apprentice: a trainee craftsman

Apprenticeship: training in a craft or trade lasting seven years

Arab empire: the area of the Middle East and north Africa ruled by Arabs

Armada: the Spanish word for a fleet of ships

Assassinate: murder for political reasons

Astrology: a belief that the movement of the planets and stars affects human lives

Banns: an announcement of marriage

BCE: Before Common Era

Benefit: gain, do well

Blood relative: a relative of the royal family by birth

Burgesses: mostly rich merchants in the towns.

Caliph: a Muslim ruler

Cause: the reason why an event happened

Cavalry: soldiers on horseback

CE: common era – the years since the time of Jesus

Census: a survey carried out every ten years about the people living in this country

Charge and discharge: load and fire

Charter: a written grant of rights by a king or queen

Chronicle: a book recording events that happened year by year

Chronological order: putting events into the order they happened

Civil war: a war fought between groups within the same country

Comet: an object in the night sky, like a star with a long tail of light

Consequence: what happens after an event

Contemporaries: people who were alive at the same time as the person being described

Continuity: when things stay the same

Corrupt: rotten or dishonest

Cruck: the main frames of a house, set in a row

Crusade: a holy war to conquer Jerusalem

Crusades: a series of wars between Christians and Muslims

Demon: an evil spirit or devil

Dissolve: used here, this means to close a monastery and take away its possessions

Diverse: different

Diversity: when people are different

Domesday Book: a report on all the land and wealth of England put together by William I in 1086–87

Doom: judgement for sinners

Early modern: the period of history from about 1500 to 1800

Ease: relaxation, comfort

Elected: voted for

Endow: give money to maintain something

Epidemic: major outbreak of a disease

Excommunicated: expelled from the church

Feudal system: a system of giving out land in return for services and loyalty

Freemen: people who were free in law and did not 'belong' to a lord

Gentry: people just below the nobility (earls, lords etc.) in social rank

Guild: an organisation to which all the craftsmen in a trade belonged

Harrying of the North: The word 'harry' means to destroy

Heaven: where the souls of good people went after purgatory

Hell: where the souls of bad people went

Heir: the person most likely to become king or queen after the monarch dies

Heretic: a person who challenges the beliefs and ideas of the church

Holy Land: lands around Jerusalem associated with Jesus and Mohammad

Hostility: bad feeling

House of correction: a prison

Houses of Parliament: the building where the important people who run the country meet to make decisions

Human rights: fair treatment for all

Hypothesis: a prediction of what might happen

Illegitimate: a child whose parents are not married and who cannot inherit a title such as 'king' from the father

Interpretation: how something is understood, a way of describing it

Jerusalem: a city that is holy for Jews, Christians and Muslims

Jetty: The over hanging upper floor of a medieval town house

Jihad: Holy War

Knights: By 1265 this meant the wealthy landowners of the counties

Legitimate heir: a child of the king and queen who could by law become the next ruler

Leper: a person who suffers from an infectious blood disease called leprosy

Life expectancy: how long people lived, on average

Magna Carta: the great charter of rights that was drawn up in 1215

Mahout: a man who looked after a working elephant

Martyr: a person who is killed for their beliefs

Mass: Catholic church service

Medieval: in the Middle Ages

Midden: a heap of human and animal dung

Mint: make a coin

Model Parliament: the parliament that met in 1295

Monarch: a king or queen

Mongols: warriors from central Asia with a fierce reputation

Motte and bailey: This was the type of castle built by the Normans after 1066.

Musketeers: soldiers with guns

Ordnance: guns of various sizes

Our Lady: Mary, the mother of Jesus

Pardon: a certificate reducing the number of years in purgatory

Pardoner: a man who sells 'pardons'

Parish: the area under the authority of the local church

Parliament: a meeting of Lords and Commons to advise the king

Parliamentarian: a Member of Parliament

Peasant: a poor medieval farmer

Persecute: treat someone unfairly and badly

Pestilence: deadly outbreak of disease

Pilgrimage: a journey to a holy place such as Jerusalem

Plotters: the men involved in organising the Gunpowder Plot

Policy: a political plan

Pomp: magnificence, grandeur

Protestant: a Christian from western Europe who rejected the teaching of the Catholic Church

Purgatory: where the souls of good people went for years, to make up for their sins

Qamargah: a large fenced-off area in which animals were hunted

Quakers: a religious group that began just after the Civil War

Queen consort: wife of a king

Rebellion: a violent protest when ordinary people attack the rulers

Reeve: a peasant appointed by the lord to supervise work on his land

Refugee: a person leaving their country to escape ill-treatment or famine

Regent: someone who rules in the place of the king

Renaissance: rebirth of learning

Shell: an explosive fired from an artillery gun

Shield wall: a wall of shields held by soldiers standing shoulder to shoulder

Significant: important

Social class: a group with similar jobs and income

Source: an object or a piece of writing from the past that helps an historian to answer his or her questions about the past

Succession: the way the right to rule is passed on to the next in line

Swivel: a type of gun

Tenant: a person who received land in return for services and loyalty

Tommy: a nickname given to British soldiers

Treason: a crime against the king or queen

Treasurer: person responsible for taking care of finances

Truce: an agreement to end fighting

Vagabond: a person with no home, a wandering beggar

Vagrant: wandering beggar

Villein: a male peasant who had to do work for the lord in exchange for being allowed to farm land for himself

Virtue: good kind of behaviour

Wantonness: loose or shameful living

Witan: council of nobles and churchmen who advised the king

Workhouse: place where poor homeless people were sent if they were caught begging

Index

Index

Index

Acknowledgements

The publishers gratefully acknowledge the permission granted to reproduce the copyright material in this book. While every effort has been made to trace and contact copyright holders, where this has not been possible the publishers will be pleased to make the necessary arrangements at the first opportunity.

p. 6 Hulton Collection/Getty Images; **p. 8** Topham Picturepoint/TopFoto; extract from *Kings & Queens*, by Eleanor & Herbert Farjeon, Jane Nissen Books, 1932; **p. 9** Popperfoto/Getty Images; **p. 10** WH CHOW/Shutterstock; **p. 12** AFP/Getty Images; **p. 14** Tadeusz Ibrom/Shutterstock; **p. 16** Thirsk Museum; **p. 17** Pete Jackson; **p. 18** De Agostini/Getty Images; **p. 19** David Sutherland/Getty Images; extract from *Pompeii* by Peter Connolly (OUP, 2004), (c) Peter Connolly 1979, 1990, reprinted by permission of OUP ; **p. 22** The Granger Collection/TopFoto; **p. 24** The Granger Collection/TopFoto; extract from article by Lord Beaverbrook, Evening Standard, 05/06/1956; quotation from *Alexander Fleming: The Man and the Myth*, by Gwyn Macfarlane, Watson, Little Ltd, 1984; **p. 26** Getty Images; **p. 28** The Art Archive/Musée Condé Chantilly/Gianni Dagli Orti; **p. 32** Amra Pasic/Shutterstock; **p. 33** Getty Images; **p. 36** Ullstein Bild/TopFoto; **p. 39** Topham Picturepoint/TopFoto; **p. 39** Woodmansterne/TopFoto; **p. 40** Topham Picturepoint/TopFoto; **p. 45** Topham Picturepoint/TopFoto; **p. 47** The British Library/HIP/TopFoto; **p. 48** TopFoto; **p. 54** Nashford Publishing; **p. 54** The British Library/TopFoto; **p. 57** The Granger Collection/TopFoto; **p. 58** The Granger Collection/TopFoto; **p. 60** The British Library/HIP/TopFoto; **p. 62** The Granger Collection/TopFoto; **p. 64** Webb Aviation; **p. 66** EE Images/HIP/TopFoto; **p. 68** All Saints Church, North Street, York; **p. 71** TopFoto; **p. 72** Dennis Barnes/TopFoto; **p. 74** E&E Images/HIP/TopFoto; quotation from *The Reformation and the English People*, by J.J. Scarisbrick, Blackwell, 1984; **p. 76** British Library/HIP/TopFoto; **p. 78** The Granger Collection/TopFoto; **p. 79** Extract from *The Plantagenet Chronicles*, by Elizabeth M. Hallam, Weidenfeld and Nicolson, imprint of The Orion Publishing Group, 1986; **p. 80** Getty Images; **p. 81** Lazar Mihai-Bogdan/Shutterstock; **p. 82** HIP/TopFoto; **p. 84** The Art Archive/National Library Cairo/Gianni Dagli Orti; **p. 85** The Art Archive/National Library Cairo/Gianni Dagli Orti; **p. 86** The Art Archive/Pharaonic Village Cairo/Gianni Dagli Orti; **p. 87** Spanish School, (13th century)/Monasterio de El Escorial, El Escorial, Spain/Index/The Bridgeman Art Library; **p. 88** The Stapleton Collection/The Bridgeman Art Library/TopFoto; quotation from *The Crusades*, by Terry Jones & Alan Ereira, BBC Books, 1994; **p. 90** Mark R. Thomas/Getty Images; quotation from Dr. Mike Ibeji, 'King John and Richard I: Brothers and Rivals', *British History in-depth*, URL http://www.bbc.co.uk/history/british/middle_ages/john_01.shtml, accessed 05/11/2009; **p. 92** UK City Images/TopFoto; **p. 94** The Granger Collection/TopFoto; **p. 96** British Library Board/The Bridgeman Art Library; **p. 97** British Library Board/The Bridgeman Art Library/TopFoto; **p. 98** The Art Archive/Saint Sebastian Chapel Lanslevillard Savoy/Gianni Dagli Orti; **p. 100** Quotation from *Medieval Lives*, by Terry Jones, BBC Books, 2005; **p. 101** The British Library/HIP/TopFoto; **p. 102** French School (14th century)/British Library/The Bridgeman Art Library; **p. 101** The Art Archive/Museo Correr Venice/Alfredo Dagli Orti; **p. 102** French School (13th century)/Bibliotheque Municipale, Agen, France/The Bridgeman Art Library; **p. 101** HIP/The British Library/TopFoto; **p. 103** The Art Archive/Biblioteca Nacional Lisbon/Gianni Dagli Orti; **p. 104** Ullstein Bild/TopFoto; **p. 108** The Granger Collection/TopFoto; **p. 111** The Art Archive/Bibliothèque de l'Arsenal Paris/Kharbine-Tapabor/Coll. Jean Vigne; **p. 112** The Granger Collection/TopFoto; **p. 114** The British Library/HIP/TopFoto; **p. 116** English Heritage Photo Library; **p. 117** Extract from 'A Fourteenth-Century Chronicle from the Grey Friars at Lynn', by Antonia Grasden, *English Historical Review*, OUP, 1957; **p. 118** The Art Archive/Bibliothèque Nationale Paris; **p. 121** English Heritage Photo Library; **p. 122** Topham Picturepoint/TopFoto; **p. 124** TopFoto; **p. 127** English School/Getty Images ; **p. 128** The British Library/HIP/TopFoto; **p. 130** French School/Getty Images; **p. 132** Sudeley Castle, Winchcombe/The Bridgeman Art Library; **p. 134** Ullstein Bild/TopFoto; **p. 135** Ann Ronan Picture Library/HIP/TopFoto; **p. 136** Extract from *The Idea of an Historical Education*, by Geoffrey Partington, NFER, 1980; **p. 138** TopFoto; **p. 140** The Art Archive/Musée du Château de Versailles/Gianni Dagli Orti; **p. 142** Edward Hawkins Collection/British Museum; **p. 143** Gerlach Flicke/Getty Images; **p. 143** The Trustees of the Weston Park Foundation/The Bridgeman Art Library; **p. 144** Ullstein Bild/TopFoto; **p. 144** English School, (16th century)/National Portrait Gallery, London, UK/The Bridgeman Art Library; **p. 146** UPPA/TopFoto; **p. 148** SuperStock/Getty Images; **p. 150** English School/Getty Images; **p. 152** English School/Getty Images; **p. 154** The Granger Collection/TopFoto; **p. 156** UK City Images/TopFoto; **p. 158** British Library Board/The Bridgeman Art Library; **p. 160** The Granger Collection/TopFoto; **p. 162** Holger Mette/Shutterstock; **p. 163** Topham Picturepoint/TopFoto; **p. 164** The Granger Collection/TopFoto; **p. 166** Istock; **p. 169** The Art Archive; **p. 171** The Art Archive/Jarrold Publishing; **p. 172** The Art Archive/British Museum; **p. 173** Poem 'Lament', by Iain Lom, from *Scotlands Poets and the Nation*, by Alan Riach/Douglas Gifford, Carcarnet Press, 2004; **p. 174** Extract (c) Oxford, Bodleian Library, MS. Carte 25, fol. 509r; **p. 175** The Art Archive/Private Collection/Philip Mould; **p. 176** World History Archive/TopFoto; **p. 177** World History Archive/TopFoto; **p. 178** World History Archive/TopFoto; **p. 178** World History Archive/TopFoto; **p. 179** The Art Archive/Handel Museum Halle/Alfredo Dagli Orti; **p. 180** The Art Archive/Handel Museum Halle/Alfredo Dagli Orti; **p. 180** Ann Ronan Picture Library/HIP/TopFoto; **p. 181** World History Archive/TopFoto; **p. 182** Roy Rainford/Getty Images; **p. 184** Fotomas/TopFoto; **p. 187** English School/Getty Images; **p. 189** British Library Board/Bridgeman Art Library; **p. 190** English School, (16th century)/Private Collection/The Bridgeman Art Library; **p. 193** English School, (16th century)/Private Collection/The Bridgeman Art Library; **p. 194** English School, (16th century)/Private Collection/The Bridgeman Art Library; **p. 197** Pete Jackson; **p. 200** English School, (17th century)/Private Collection/The Bridgeman Art Library; **p. 203** The British Library Board, E.1150.(5.); **p. 205** Getty Images; **p. 206** Getty Images; **p. 210** TopFoto; **p. 211** Roy Rainford/TopFoto; **p. 213** Peter Willi/Getty Images; **p. 214** Ironbridge Gorge Museum/The Bridgeman Art Library